SEVEN B
That Make Life Work

phil pringle

SEVEN BIG THINGS
That Make Life Work

Principles
for
Successful
Living

phil pringle

DESTINY IMAGE® PUBLISHERS, INC.

P.O. Box 310, Shippensburg, PA 17257-0310

"Speaking to the Purposes of God for This Generation and for the Generations to Come."

This book and all other Destiny Image, Revival Press, MercyPlace, Fresh Bread, Destiny Image Fiction, and Treasure House books are available at Christian bookstores and distributors worldwide.

For a U.S. bookstore nearest you, call 1-800-722-6774.

For more information on foreign distributors, call 717-532-3040.

Reach us on the Internet: www.destinyimage.com.

Trade Paper ISBN 13: 978-0-7684-3245-9
Hardcover ISBN: 978-0-7684-3467-5
Large Print ISBN: 978-0-7684-3468-2
E-book ISBN: 978-0-7684-9106-7

For Worldwide Distribution, Printed in the U.S.A.
1 2 3 4 5 6 7 8 9 / 14 13 12 11 10

COMMENTS ON THE WORKS OF
PHIL PRINGLE

One thing is for sure…this world needs leaders who operate with excellence! Dr. Pringle's *Top 10 Qualities of a Great Leader* aims at the heart of a leader, giving you both spiritual and practical insights that will radically change the way you lead.

Joyce Meyer
Best-selling author and Bible teacher

God's blessings are released when we give from generous and willing hearts. *Keys to Financial Excellence,* by my friend, Pastor Phil Pringle, reveals God's desire not only to meet our needs, but also to pour out His abundance. Topics such as the blessing of tithing, debt cancellation, the laws of giving, and sowing to the Spirit will awaken in you a desire to transform the world through the power of giving.

John Bevere
Best-selling author and Bible teacher

Dr. Phil Pringle has written one of the clearest, most biblical works on leadership I have ever read. It is comprehensive and compelling. Reading it motivated me to go to the next level in my own leadership. Thanks, Phil.

Bill Hybels, Senior Pastor
Willow Creek Community Church

Leadership is a hot topic, and for good reason—we've never needed good leaders more than today. In a world overrun with principles, ideals, and wish lists about leadership, it is refreshing to hear from a practicing, effective, productive, and influential leader. And a leader who isn't driven by the bottom line, but by people and their development and well-being. Years of consistency and fruitfulness have penned these pages.

Kong Hee, Senior Minister
City Harvest Church
Singapore

It's always a great pleasure to read material that has been tried and proven by the author. Phil Pringle is one of those leaders of a rare breed who writes from the fiery furnace of experience. He has sown these principles of financial wisdom into countless thousands of people and hundreds of churches. *Keys to Financial Excellence* will change your financial life if you put them into practice. This material is great for all levels of people: the business person, the person seeking to get out of debt, the pastor who has vision but not enough resources, the young person who desires to set their financial path before them, and the giver in every church who desires to go to another level of giving and receiving. This book is a winner. It's trustworthy, biblical, practical, and inspirational.

Frank Damazio
City Bible Church

Keys to Financial Excellence isn't a book written from an ideological perspective—it's the real stuff, tried and proven…for people who want wisdom in a world of conflicting messages.

John C. Maxwell
Best-selling author

Phil Pringle's outstanding leadership skills have been proven over many years, and so he is well-qualified to write this exceptional book on leadership.

Pastor Brian Houston, Senior Minister
Hillsong Church
Sydney, Australia

God has the perfect answers for us in every situation if we will simply ask Him! These times of unusual challenges call for renewed hope in Christ. Pastor Phil Pringle's *The Art of Prayer* paints a lyrical picture of how our lives can be dramatically transformed if we will only pray to God and trust that He has great plans for us!

Bishop T.D. Jakes Sr.
The Potter's House of Dallas

Phil Pringle is a true leader of leaders. He has a fresh, unique way of looking at everything, and there is a strong anointing on his life and ministry. He writes from a wealth of knowledge and experience.

Pastor Rick Shelton
Senior Minister, Life Christian Center
St. Louis, Missouri

I would like to recommend *You the Leader* by Dr. Phil Pringle. All true Christians are called to use their talents and gifts in a position of authority in the Body of Christ. This book will help each Christian understand his or her role in the Body.

Dr. David Yonggi Cho
The Yoido Full Gospel Church
Seoul, South Korea

There is no doubt that Phil Pringle is one of the most outstanding Christian leaders in the world today. His vision, passion, influence, and ministry impact over many decades attest to that. Through this book you have the opportunity to glean wisdom and insights from his life and journey. I heartily recommend it!

Mark Conner, Senior Minister
CityLife Church

Phil Pringle has been at the forefront of radical church leadership for many years. At Christian City Church, he has pioneered many different areas of ministry, gleaning valuable insight and wisdom along the way.

Pastor Colin Dye, Senior Minister
Kensington Temple
London, England

Inspiring, thought-provoking, challenging.

Russell Evans, Director
Planet Shakers, South Australia

Dr. Phil Pringle is a gifted leader who is being used to inspire and provoke people all around the world. I have had the privilege of speaking at conferences with him and have watched how his motivational messages have impacted a generation. I highly recommend this book to anyone who wants to be a world changer!

Matthew Barnett, Senior Pastor
The Dream Center
Los Angeles, California

What a wonderful name for our dear friend Dr. Phil Pringle's masterpiece, *The Art of Prayer*. Dr. Pringle is a great writer and he is also a wonderful artist. In his new book, he has combined both of these gifts to create a great work of literature and art. …This book is the best of two worlds and it discusses every possible subject connected with prayer in a most artistic manner. Enjoy *The Art of Prayer* and be blessed. You will view prayer in a new dimension.

Dr. David Yonggi Cho
The Yoido Full Gospel Church
Seoul, South Korea

Phil Pringle is one of the few leaders who knows how to mentor others. …*You the Leader* is crammed full of extraordinary insights that will help you become the dynamic leader God wants you to be. I highly recommend it.

C. Peter Wagner
Wagner Leadership Institute

The Art of Prayer is an eloquent and much-needed reminder that there is nothing we cannot rise above as long as we keep the path of communication flowing between ourselves and God. As Phil Pringle so beautifully demonstrates in this unique and lyrical book, one of the most empowering ways to abide in God's will is through prayer.

Kenneth Ulmer, Senior Pastor
Faithful Central Bible Church
Los Angeles, California

A much needed prod to remind us of the call to come before the Almighty God in prayer. Through his enthralling creativeness and authenticity, Phil Pringle lays down many amazing principles and truths apropos of prayer in this masterpiece.

Kong Hee
City Harvest Church

Phil Pringle is one of the most influential leaders of our time. He has a burning passion and zeal for the lost and hurting. This book will change your view on prayer, how to communicate with God, and will bless you in an amazing way!

Pastor Matthew Barnett
Dream Center
Los Angeles, California

CONTENTS

—

PREFACE

*...though by this time you ought to be teachers, you
need someone to teach you again the first principles of
the oracles of God; and you have come to need milk and
not solid food. For everyone who partakes only of milk is
unskilled in the word of righteousness, for he is a babe.
But solid food belongs to those who are of full age, that
is, those who by reason of use have their senses exer-
cised to discern both good and evil (Hebrews 5:12-14
NKJV).*

THESE STUDIES OF THE FOUNDATIONS of your Christian life cover
the seven topics strung together in chapter 6 of the New Testament Book of Hebrews. These key principles are the root of your life in
Christ. When new believers don't get these fundamentals, they struggle
to live their life in victory.

These studies relate very specifically to leaders. Every leader must
have a firm grasp of each spiritual reality presented here, because *we
simply cannot lead people to where we ourselves have never been!*

These truths did not take root in my own life until after I had truly met Christ—long after I became a Christian. Sometimes we hear teachings that seem to say that we must clean our lives up *before* we are able to receive Christ and begin our walk with God. But *that's untrue*. Fish are not gutted and cleaned until after they're caught. The man in the Matthew 13 parable *first* found the pearl of great price and *then* went and sold all he had in order to acquire it; and the other man *first* discovered the treasure in the field and *then*, "for joy" over what he had found, went and sold all he had so he could buy the field. That is what following Christ is all about. We *first discover Him* and we *then put our lives in order*, with His help and power.

The foundations presented here ensure that all believers remain in the Kingdom of God after we have received Christ and are born again. Without these first principles, we are unable to progress in God. Our growth will be stunted and the call of God will fail to be realized. These are the basics. Without them, we are unable to cope with the further truths for mature Christianity. These essentials, the "milk" of young Christianity, are what prepare us for the "strong meat" of adulthood in Christ.

INTRODUCTION

Foundations

Therefore let us leave the elementary teachings about Christ and go on to maturity, not laying again the foundation of repentance from acts that lead to death, and of faith in God (Hebrews 6:1 NIV).

THE TRUE CHRISTIAN LEADER HAS a firm grasp on the basics of Christian living. He knows he cannot take people where he himself has not been. If he does not live in the truths of the Scripture he teaches, then he neither knows the way nor how to get there. For example, if a leader has not passed through repentance, he or she will be unable to lead anyone else there or effectively teach the tenets, the purpose, and the effects of repentance.

Without foundations, a building cannot remain standing. The same applies to our lives. The Christian life crumbles without a correct foundation. This foundation is a combination of actions, attitudes, beliefs, and practices that must be put into place immediately after conversion.

GOING ON

In the first verse of Hebrews chapter 6, the writer enjoins us to "go on" to maturity and to "leave" the elementary teachings regarding Christ that the writer discussed in the preceding five chapters of Hebrews. In this passage, the Greek word for *leave* is *aphiemi*, which along with a variety of interpretations also means "to send forth, in various applications such as 'to follow'."[1] Thus, once we begin applying the basics of biblical behavior to our lives, we keep progressing, applying the further teachings of Christ.

Verse 3 then reveals something very interesting: our progress in the Kingdom will only occur under permission from God. In other words, if certain principles are not learned, the Christian is not equipped with the necessary "tools" for the challenges of a more mature Christian lifestyle. For example:

- If I do not complete today's homework, then I will not be able to deal with tomorrow's world.

- If I do not cope with the trials and application of truth, then I am ill-equipped to deal with the real world God is asking me to influence.

- If I have not learned faith today, then I will not be able to take God's people into Canaan tomorrow—and, because "Canaan"

will be conquered by faith alone, I will be
a dead spy, lying lifeless on the sands of
Sinai, instead of like Joshua and Caleb,
vibrant forty years on and "conquering
kingdoms."

DIG DEEP

*Whoever comes to Me, and hears My sayings and does them, I
will show you whom he is like: "He is like a man building a
house, who dug deep and laid the foundation on the rock. And
when the flood arose, the stream beat vehemently against that
house, and could not shake it, for it was founded on the rock.
"But he who heard and did nothing is like a man who built
a house on the earth without a foundation, against which the
stream beat vehemently; and immediately it fell. And the ruin
of that house was great"* (Luke 6:47-49 NKJV).

William Barclay tells us that during the summer months in Pales-
tine, rivers would often run dry.[2] For the uninitiated, the long stretches
of sand were appealing areas to build a house. However, as winter arrived, the unsuspecting new inhabitants would find themselves and
their homes swept away by the flood of water filling the riverbed once
again.

In Luke 6:47-49, Jesus explains that the house built on rock will
stand. He says the man "dug deep," separating all the dirt from between himself and the rock in order to lay the foundation on the rock.
Obviously, the rock is Christ. He is not discovered by the casual hearer.
Neither does a life become successful when built on sand or dirt. If
Christians do not take time to *dig deep* and lay the correct foundation,
their lives will topple when turbulence comes.

LAYING A SOLID FOUNDATION

There are seven principles that lay a solid foundation for Christian living:

- Repentance

- Faith Toward God

- Baptisms

- Spiritual Gifts

- Laying on of Hands

- Resurrection of the Dead

- Eternal Judgment

There are many reasons why people fail to lay this crucial foundation—and find themselves constantly wondering why their Christian walk is weak and ineffective. Here are just a few reasons people fail to dig deep and lay a proper foundation:

> - Some people have a very short-term view of their walk with God. They want their house up *today*. They're impatient. They give little thought to the future. Their impetuosity gets the better of sound advice. They build upward in the visible arena, which, to them, is far more satisfying than the hard work required to build a foundation that no one can see. For

example, young Christians who rise too quickly into ministry, possibly because of a sensational testimony or personal or professional connections, must apply themselves to laying the unseen foundation of prayer and study in their lives. If they don't, the pressures of public notoriety bear down on their character and they will lose their purpose—and possibly even more. Pride comes easy to an unrepentant heart. Sins that have not been fully dealt with grow into deep flaws that will plague one's reputation and eventually destroy a believer's life.

- Laziness. Some people avoid hard work or work that doesn't show instant reward. They only want to do what they consider the "bare necessities." They are unprepared to pay the price of a solid life, and unconcerned if it wobbles along. Getting life "right" is too hard on their emotions and character.

- Some people simply don't see the importance of laying a solid foundation. Their time is "too valuable" to spend on prayer, on Bible study, on seeking God. This essential foundation is unimportant to them. To them, to "appear" to be doing the right thing is enough; to actually be "right," however, is another matter.

In the following chapters we are going to examine each of the seven foundational principles for effective, flourishing, successful Christian living. These principles will prepare you to be ready to accelerate into your future.

> *Brothers, I could not address you as spiritual but as worldly—mere infants in Christ. I gave you milk, not solid food, for you were not yet ready for it. Indeed, you are still not ready. You are still worldly...* (1 Corinthians 3:1-3 NIV).

ENDNOTES

1. *Strong's Dictionary,* G863; aphiemi.

2. William Barclay, *Daily Study Bible* (Akron, OH: St. Andrews Press, 1955).

Repentance

THE FIRST LAYER OF OUR foundation is "repentance from dead works." To *repent* is to respond to the conviction of the Holy Spirit. Repentance is possibly our greatest gift from God. Without it, we cannot be saved.

Before we can repent, however, *conviction* must come. Conviction is the awakening of a person's conscience to the truth and reality of his or her own state of sinfulness. This happens best in the climate of the presence of God. Whether He is revealed in judgment, goodness, greatness, power, or love, the revelation will highlight shortcomings in our lives.

Real preaching brings *conviction.* Under this conviction, the people must be allowed to break and to confess their sins to God. If they are comforted prematurely, they fail to experience the full breakthrough that repentance brings. Assurance of freedom from sin should come into the heart from within, not from without. In other words, a counselor should not be the source of initial assurance. Only the Holy

Spirit is able to witness within as to whether the heart is free from sin, cleansed, and made righteous by God, as apostle Paul points in Romans 8:16: *"The Spirit Himself bears witness with our spirit that we are children of God."*

For example, in Luke 5 when apostle Peter is told by Christ to *"launch out into the deep for a catch,"* Peter is hesitant, he doesn't believe this is a good idea. After all, he's an experienced, professional fisherman who has fished the lake from when he was a child. He "knows" he will catch nothing right now. He tells Jesus that he worked hard all night and caught nothing. He has cleaned his nets and is ready to go home. *"Nevertheless,"* Peter responds to the Lord, *"at Your word I will let down nets."* Does this mean that the fisherman is patronizing the Carpenter? No, he is obeying Him (albeit reluctantly). The result? Peter lands an unbelievably enormous catch.

In spite of Peter's complaining reluctance, God revealed to him His goodness, love, and power. The fisherman's response to God's blessing was conviction of, and repentance from, his downplaying of Christ's instructions. *"Depart from me Lord,"* Peter exclaims, *"for I am a sinful man."* Only in the face of an act of God did he realize his doubt of God. This is just one way God leads people to repentance. Peter's repentance dealt with a crucial facet of his life: the doubts he harbored regarding the words of Jesus.

At another time, however, in John 13:8 when Jesus was about to wash Peter's feet, Peter flat-out refused. *"Lord,"* he responded, *"You shall never wash my feet!"* Peter's inference was that the task belonged to a servant, not the Master—but that was exactly the lesson Jesus was showing. The Lord replied to Peter that those who are not washed by Him have no part in Him. So Peter said, "then wash all of me!"

In addition to other lessons, Peter was still learning to get out of the driver's seat and let Christ rule his life. Jesus implied that he who is already washed, needs only to wash his hands and feet. This is a play on words. The first word used for "washed" is the Greek word *louo*, which means "to bathe the whole body,"[1] as in a bath or a shower. The second word is *nipto*, meaning a basic washing of hands, feet, or face. The picture is that of a person washing himself completely in the public Roman baths in the center of town. While walking home however, the "washed" person may get their hands or feet grubby; so when they get home, they need only to wash their hands and feet.

Throughout our Christian life we need to wash our "hands and feet." The means by which we do this is *repentance*, a "gift" we receive when we first choose to turn from our old life. We feel shame over the sins we have committed, but we also feel hatred for sin itself. We reject our previous life—not just the "sins" of our past ways, but a whole life that was lived against God and without Christ. We repent from it. This should be an emotional experience that breaks our heart.

So many people never experience a full release into their Christian life, because they do not fully leave their old life. They do not truly repent.

> *For you know that afterward, when he wanted to inherit the blessing, he was rejected for he found no place for repentance, though he sought it diligently with tears* (Hebrews 12:17).

REPENTANCE DEFINED

The Greek word for repentance is *metanoeo*, which means "to perceive afterwards."[2] Repentance is the ability to see clearly after a sinful act and to then proceed to take the steps necessary to address and repair it. If only we felt as bad about sin *before* we committed it as we did *after*, we probably never would commit it in the first place. Without making too light of the subject, it's like eating fish and chips: they smell good and taste great, but afterward the greasy feeling of an indigestible blob in your stomach makes you wish you'd never eaten them.

WHAT REPENTANCE IS:

- True repentance is *godly sorrow over our sin*: *"Godly sorrow produces repentance leading to salvation"* (2 Cor. 7:10).

- True repentance is *confessing our sin to God*: *"I will confess my transgressions to the Lord, and You forgave the iniquity of my sin"* (Ps. 32:5); and, *"If we confess our sins, He is faithful and just to forgive us our sins and to cleanse us from all unrighteousness"* (1 John 1:9).

- True repentance is *forsaking sins*: *"... whoever confesses and forsakes them, will have mercy"* (Prov. 28:13).

- True repentance is *feeling a hatred of sin itself*, for your past sins as well as for the person who committed them—yourself: *"...you shall loathe yourselves in your own sight because of all the evils that you have committed"* (Ezek. 20:43).

WHAT REPENTANCE IS NOT:

- Repentance is *not* merely "sorrow." Apostle Paul explains in Second Corinthians 7:10 that this worldly type of sorrow *"produces death."*

- Repentance does *not* mean to just "turn over a new leaf." In Isaiah 64:6 the prophet says that human righteousness is *"like filthy rags."*

- Repentance has *nothing* to do with just becoming "religious." John the Baptist tells the Pharisees and Sadducees coming to him for baptism in Matthew 3:8 to *"bring forth fruits worthy of repentance."*

- Repentance is *not* "mental acceptance of truth." Even the devil believes in God—but it is not academic knowledge that saves, as apostle James says in James 2:19: *"You believe that there is one God. You do well. Even the demons believe—and tremble!"*

RESTITUTION

Repentance from sin produces *restitution*. The Hebrew word for restitution is *shalam* (the Greek is *apokathistemi*), which mean "to restore, to make amends, to make right what was wrong."[3] Zacchaeus did exactly this when he repaid four times the amount he had defrauded anyone.

It is crucial to help young Christians do this so they get their lives right.

In Matthew 5:48 when Jesus said we are to *"be perfect,"* He wasn't expecting us to be without any fault throughout our entire lives. He realized that would be an impossible request. What He was commanding was that we take hold of the meaning behind the Greek word for "perfect" *(teleios),* which basically means "to repair" and/or "to adjust."[4] If we are constantly willing to repair and to adjust, then we will negotiate our way through most everything successfully. This ability, this "art," is learned right in the foundational days of our Christian life, at the moment when we repent.

To "repair" is to heal what has been wounded, to recover what has been lost, to fix what has been broken. When this applies to relationships, it inevitably requires apologizing for wrongs committed. From the other side, when we have been wronged by the sins of another person, that requires us to forgive. Both of these qualities—*repair* and *adjust*—are what mend a damaged relationship.

To "adjust" is the ability to change, to escape the ruts and fixations of our lifestyle, to break old, negative habits and to form new, positive ones. People who develop this ability, Jesus considers "perfect." They *put things right.*

For example, people with stolen property in their homes need to return it. Lies we've told need to be corrected. Forgiveness should be sought from people we have wronged—from parents, family, friends, and any others. An uneasy conscience is miserable to live with. This is coming into the light. It may be difficult but this is the only way to create a solid foundation for the rest of our lives.

BREAK WITH THE WAYS OF THE WORLD

There are some areas of repentance that are better left singularly to the blood of Christ. I knew of one person who had stolen a lot of food from supermarkets. There was no way of knowing how much he had taken since he had eaten it all. It was better for him to simply confess it to God and accept forgiveness. However, he also had a book he had stolen from a shop. That, he needed to return.

Other acts of repentance include things like destroying occult paraphernalia. These should be completely removed from our homes. Music that leads us away from God should be gotten rid of. Books opposing God's ways should be thrown out.

Repentance means to *break with the ways of the world*. If I fail to do this at the beginning of the Christian life, then I have failed to dig deep and lay a correct foundation. At some later date, when I am being tempted or persecuted, the hold the world still has on me will drag me backward, out of God. The result—a backslidden Christian.

OBSTACLES TO RESTITUTION

An unrepentant heart tries to avoid restitution because it is so challenging to pride.

The unrepentant heart attempts to justify a wrong. "Everybody does it!"

Or, explain it away. "I couldn't help it!"

And on and on...

"They made me do it!"

"What else could I do?"

"I should ignore it."

"It's only a small thing."

"It happened so long ago—who'll ever know?"

These slippery avoidances leave us still with guilt eating away in our spirit like a worm in an apple.

Repentance occupies one of the primary seats of Scripture. It is the road back to God. He commands it! Over and over again we are all called to repent. John the Baptist, Jesus, and the apostles all preached repentance, and we too are commissioned with the same task: *"...repentance and remission of sins should be preached in His name to all nations..."* (Luke 24:47).

THE POWER OF REPENTANCE

Repentance is the **essential** first step in the Christian life because it brings three important things:

1. Repentance gets you ready to receive from God....*Break up your fallow ground, for it is time to seek the Lord, till He comes and rains righteousness on you* (Hosea 10:12).

If the heart does not soften and break up, it cannot receive watering and the "seed" of the Word. Water simply skates over the surface of hard ground. It's the same with the heart: if it is hard, the Spirit is unable to penetrate deeply and effect change.

Mark 4:3 tells the parable of the sower and the seed. The success of the seed (the Word of God) depends on the quality of the ground.

Stony ground, weedy ground, and rocky ground are all states of the heart that render the seed unfruitful. The seed is ruined under these conditions. Repentance is the one act that prepares the soil (the heart) for fruitfulness. It removes weeds, hardness, and apathy. Repentance fears God, so is motivated to get right with Him. Hardness is pride and a willful resistance to God. Repentance humbles the heart and surrenders to God. A hard heart is closed to God. A repentant heart is open to God.

2. Repentance keeps us in a discipleship position. *So likewise, whoever of you does not forsake all that he has **cannot** be My disciple* (Luke 14:33).

Repentance is forsaking sin, the world, and the devil. This means breaking with sinful acts. It means offloading all the bridges that connect with the world. Often this is old friends, habits, possessions, music, books, etc. Some of these things may be innocent in themselves. But because they are attached to the heart, they need to be severed from the life of the new believer. If these things are not "forsaken," they are like a handle affixed to the back of a Christian: the devil takes hold of it and pulls them straight back into the world.

3. Repentance breaks the hold of the world on us. *Now we have received, not the spirit of the world, but the Spirit who is from God...* (1 Cor. 2:12).

Once believers break with the spirit of the world, it has no more power over them. If young Christians fail to make this break with the world, they will inevitably backslide, endangering their salvation. It's impossible to follow Christ without repenting from the sins of our previous life and breaking from the world. The gift of repentance is the scalpel God has given us to accomplish this.

Deliverance from demonic power also depends upon repentance from the sin that allowed satan entrance in the first place. If the will is not set against the devil and sin, it is virtually impossible to bring freedom from demonic bondage.

BLOCKAGES TO FORGIVENESS

The true result of repentance is joy, freedom, and a close walk with God. If this doesn't take place, then something is faulty.

Blockages to receiving forgiveness are:

1. Failure to forsake sin, that is, to repent from it and choose not to repeat it, compromises our sense of forgiveness. You cannot cheat yourself. Inwardly a person knows whether they are being true or hypocritical. Just confessing sin will not bring full release from it.

2. Failure to forgive ourselves hinders the sense of God's forgiveness. People can be told that God has forgiven them, yet often they are unable to extend the same mercy to themselves. However, they must; because this is a major door through which satan continues to condemn believers.

3. Failure to forgive others will prevent the forgiveness of God from shining through to our emotions. Jesus has declared that if we do not forgive those who have offended us, then we will not be forgiven by God in Heaven (see Matt. 18:21-35). It is vital that we make a regular habit of forgiving everyone, everything, they have ever done to us.

4. Broken relationships will also trouble the assurance of forgiveness in our life. If we are aware that someone else holds a grudge against us, then the effort to repair that relationship must be made. Jesus said that before we come to worship the Father, we must make the relationship right (see Matt. 5:23-24). If we are unsuccessful, then we must put the problem from our mind and not allow it to trouble us further. We've done all we can do.

THE ATTITUDE OF REPENTANCE

...My son, do not despise the chastening of the Lord... (Hebrews 12:5).

When circumstances challenge you, keep a great attitude! Mature people show great attitude when they're "adjusted." The ability to accept correction is the doorway to progress. Owning a great attitude when you're being given instruction you're uncomfortable with is a key to growth. If you throw tantrums, sulk, or try to "get even," you won't grow, and you'll still have the fault that caused the problem in the first place.

The presence of God is extraordinary. We carry it with us all the time. If we are careful about the way we live, the Holy Spirit remains the undisputed Lord in our lives. His power manifests around us continually. This power manifests and affects others when we focus our faith on realities Christ has placed within us:

that the sharing of your faith may become effective by the acknowledgement of every good thing which is in you in Christ Jesus (Philemon 1:6).

"Acknowledging every good thing *in* us," we release those same things *through* us. This applies equally in the negative. People who constantly acknowledge weakness live weak lives. Constantly recalling our failures, sins, and shortcomings defeats us. We should repent from these things when we need to. But that's it. Repentance is a doorway, not a living room. Once repented of, we accept forgiveness from the Father and cleansing by the blood of Jesus. We move on. We acknowledge those grand qualities God placed in us by grace.

You are of God, little children, and have overcome them, because He who is in you is greater than he who is in the world (1 John 4:4).

My wife, Chris, and I dealt with many drug addicts in our early Christian days. One young man came to our door in the middle of the night. He was addicted to pelfium (a synthetic heroin). Although he was heavily "stoned," the Holy Spirit had moved on him to come to our home. Knowing we were "religious," and he in fact was completely adverse to Christianity, he stayed home, locked his bedroom door, put the key on the shelf, and hoped the insane notion would pass. He sat on his bed playing his guitar.

However, the compulsion to come to our house intensified. Conviction increased. In desperation he threw the key out the window! Eventually he couldn't take it anymore. He climbed out the window and ran to our house! We recognized "Who" sent him our way. After talking about Jesus, we went back to his place, found his drugs, and destroyed them.

We all returned to our house and he sat in a chair in the living room—without moving—for two days. During that time the Holy Spirit completely delivered him from addiction. We asked many times if he wanted to get up and eat something. He replied he was too afraid to move, in case the feeling of the peace of God left him.

> *Repent therefore and be converted, that your sins may be blotted out, so that times of refreshing may come from the presence of the Lord* (Acts 3:19).

The meaning of the word *refreshing*, (Greek, *anapsuxis*), literally means "a recovery of breath, revival, cooling, refreshing, recovery from the effects of heat."[4] It was only after truly, fully repenting from his drug use that that young man was caught by the powerful, refreshing presence of God and overcame his addiction.

ENDNOTES

1. *Strong's Dictionary,* #3068.

2. *Strong's Dictionary,* #3340.

3. *Strong's Dictionary,* #G600.

4. *Strong's Dictionary,* #G403.

FOUNDATION TWO

Faith Toward God

ONCE WE HAVE **"DUG DEEP"** through repentance, we can then lay the first substantial building block of the foundation: *faith*. The Greek word for faith is *pistis*. *Young's Concordance* says that this word means "substratum...that which is under."[1] Faith is a deep confidence, a firm assurance. It is the foundation.

THE WORD

Faith is inextricably linked with the Word of God. The foundation for any building must mesh with the solid base under it. Faith welds us to Christ, and He is the Word of God. Faith draws its life from the Word, which is Christ.

> *In the beginning was the Word and the Word was with God and the Word was God. And the Word became flesh and dwelt among us...* (John 1:1,14).

Faith in God, then, is the foundation for the Christian. This is fantastic, because this means the foundation of our lives is a positive, bright, sunny attitude!

FOUNDATIONAL FAITH

Foundational faith deals basically with the believer's assurance of salvation. However, as we follow Christ, we are in a perpetual process of growth. Each stage calls for us to take a fresh look at fundamental issues. Every new stage requires that we revisit the foundation of our life. This means we repent from those things hindering our progress. It also means that we go to a higher level of faith as we possess more of the land ahead.

- Repentance is a doorway.

- Faith is a living room. Faith is what we "live" by.

- Repentance clears away unwanted rubble.

- Faith builds a new life.

- Repentance is removing all the dirt between our self and the Rock, Jesus, where our faith rests.

Again, leaders cannot take anyone where they have not been themselves, for they do not know the destination nor do they know the way. Simply "knowing" about faith is not enough. *Exercising* faith is what it is all about. The men and women who practice faith are those who will not only be able to speak about it clearly, but also show those they lead how it's done.

THE HEART IS A BELIEVING MACHINE

For with the heart one believes... (Romans 10:10).

The reason repentance must occur prior to faith is that the heart is the believing machine of the human being. If the heart remains blocked with sinfulness, pride, and hateful attitudes, it cannot hold faith in the same environment. All resentment, lack of forgiveness, sin, etc., must be washed away through a sorrowful attitude that brings the blood of Jesus and the forgiveness of God into the believer's life.

The heart can only be occupied with one major emotion at any given time. Our heart is either for God or against Him. It is either loving or hating. It is either believing or doubting. Repentance clears the way for faith to arrive—and it is vital that faith is present, for:

Without faith it is impossible to please Him... (Hebrews 11:6).

...whatever is not from faith is sin (Romans 14:23).

...you have been saved through faith... (Ephesians 2:8).

RECEIVING THE WORD

Faith is formed in our hearts by the Word of God. We receive the Word by five different means:

1. *Hearing* the Word

2. *Reading* the Word

3. *Studying* the Word

4. *Memorizing* the Word

5. *Meditating* on the Word

Job 23:12 says that the Word of God should be among the primary delights of our lives: *"I have treasured the words of His mouth more than my necessary food."* If the Word is the primary delight of our lives, we will attend to it and feed on it every day we live.

> *My son, give attention to my words; incline your ear to my sayings. Do not let them depart from your eyes; keep them in the midst of your heart* (Proverbs 4:20-21).

Let me repeat: faith is formed in our hearts by the entrance of God's Word. Romans 10:17 teaches, *"faith comes by hearing, and hearing by the word of God."*

EVERYONE HAS FAITH

Many people think they have no faith. Not true! According to Romans 12:3 everyone is born with faith, *"God has dealt to each one a measure of faith."* In fact, the inner man *operates by faith*.

Faith is a spirit faculty (see Heb. 11). Faith contacts the spiritual world, which the natural person cannot. We have a duplicate set of spirit faculties in our inner spirit than those we have in our physical self. When we are born again, we receive a newly created spirit person. This new creation can "see," can "feel," can "taste," can "smell," and can "hear."

Faith deals with the unseen and the unfelt. It deals with the future and the desires of the heart. It provides "evidence" and "title deed" of things that are invisible.

Faith provides the substantiation of things that are unfelt by any of our "physical world" senses. This substance is spirit substance. It is interpreted by our emotions and mind as something we just *know*.

Faith is divine assurance planted in our inner selves by the Word of God. You do not require faith for what you can see and feel; you require faith *for what you cannot see and cannot feel*.

All of us are accustomed to basing our perceptions of reality on what our five natural senses have told us. The Kingdom of God runs on entirely different principles. A new consciousness enters our lives the moment we are born of the Spirit. A *spirit consciousness* awakens. This is a "knowing" of things that is not based on sight or feel or sometimes even logic, but rather on the Word of God. This Word lives in our inner spirit.

The substance of the spiritual reality is imparted into the believer's consciousness. We must learn to base our actions on this knowledge, because this knowledge *is the truth!* Often, natural feelings and circumstances will contradict the inner witness. But this is exactly why faith exists. We take steps (that is, we walk) by faith, not by sight.

FAITH CONTACTS GRACE

After repenting from sin, we must move quickly into a position of faith. Otherwise, our awakened conscience will overwhelm us with guilt. This guilt will not allow feelings of forgiveness to surface, but rather a conscience-driven agenda. A conscience-driven life attempts to get right and stay right with God by *works*. This operates from a premise that it is what we do or do not do that merits the favor or disfavor of God.

That is the most faulty of all foundations! We are saved by *grace* through faith, not by our own merit. Not by doing. Not by works.

There is nothing we can do or not do to earn salvation. It has already all been done by the work of Christ on the cross at Calvary.

THE ELEMENTS OF SALVATION FAITH

So, what exactly is this "salvation"? What are the elements of the work of grace? What is it that we have received? The answers to these questions are the very core of our walk with God. If we stray from these elements, or if we never fully understand them, the life we build will not survive the onslaught of the devil.

Salvation faith appropriates five things:

1. Forgiveness

2. Justification

3. Sonship

4. Sanctification

5. Redemption

Let's examine each.

1. FORGIVENESS

You are forgiven. Once you have repented from sin, you have been forgiven by God, whether you feel it or not. First John 1:9 says, *"If we confess our sins, He is faithful and just to forgive us our sins and to cleanse us from all unrighteousness."*

The biggest problem most of us face in this area is forgiving *ourselves*. Reliving the incident will not purge our souls from sin. Feeling bad about it will not do it. Only one thing can cleanse the stain of sin from the soul—the blood of Jesus.

The power of the blood of Jesus is released when we place faith in it. You may say, "But I don't *feel* forgiven." The truth is that you *are* forgiven the moment you repent from sin, ask forgiveness, and believe God's Word. If this truth does not become embedded in a person's life, he or she becomes dogged with condemnation every time they slip. Trying to live in joy and victory with a condemning conscience is impossible. Satan gains access to the mind through this weakness. He accuses us of our sin day and night, keeping us discouraged and powerless—unless we choose to believe that the Blood has cleansed us.

Now understand that, just as it says in Luke 8:11, the Word is the "seed." This means that you can grow whatever you want in your life simply by planting the seed in your heart. If you want to grow apples, you don't plant pear seeds. Likewise, if you need assurance of forgiveness, don't read just anything in Scripture, read what the Word of God declares about *forgiveness*. As you meditate upon the "seed/Word," it will digest in your soul and the light of its truth will dawn like the morning sun.

You see, faith comes by hearing the Word of God. To increase your faith, *speak* the Scripture passage that applies to you. Faith will enter your soul. This faith empowers you to believe the Scripture in an even more complete way. This is one of the most powerful spiritual cycles to engage in. Isaiah 43:22-26 reveals that God is more interested in forgiving us than in remembering our sins. He tells us to *forget* the former things and instead, *"Put **Me** in remembrance,"* He says in Isaiah 43:26, *"State your case, that you may be acquitted."*

Ephesians 1:7 emphasizes, *"In Him we have...the forgiveness of sins...."* Part of our covenant right with God is forgiveness. Forgiveness is something we simply *have*. It is part of our inheritance. When we need forgiveness, it is available. When we confess our sin, we receive forgiveness. It *belongs* to us. Thank God!

2. JUSTIFICATION

We have righteousness. To be declared righteous is to be justified. The Greek word translated as *justify* is *dikaioo*. It means "to render, show, regard as, or declare righteous."[2]

Job asks the question in Job 9:2: *"how can a man be righteous* [just] *before God?"* His question is answered in Habakkuk 2:4, Romans 1:17, and Galatians 3:11. God saw that this truth is so vital that it bears repeating three times in Scripture as a quote, and then it is expounded time and again by apostle Paul as he lays the doctrinal foundation for the Church: *"The just shall live by faith."* That is how we are righteous before God.

The greatest problem Paul faced was removing the basis for salvation from the works of the Old Testament law and replacing that with Christ. This was Paul's challenge because the Old Testament was completely the opposite: it declared that the only way to secure righteousness was to fully obey all the law of Moses. This "way of salvation" had been reinforced generation after generation. Now Paul faced the extraordinary challenge of tearing it down and presenting them with something brand-new—something that was an anathema to the traditional Hebrew: justification by faith. However, Paul held the line, and in Romans 3:28 declared, *"Therefore we conclude that a man is justified by faith apart from the deeds of the law."*

Again, "to justify" means "to declare righteous." Jeremiah 23:6 reveals in capital letters that there will come a day when God will be known as: *"THE LORD OUR RIGHTEOUSNESS"* (NKJV). This is one of the compound Hebrew names God chose to reveal Himself by in the Old Testament: *Jehovah Tsidkenu*, which literally means, "The Lord our righteousness."[3] This single statement contains one of the most fantastic revelations of salvation in the entire Bible. It was not until the New Testament dawned that the truth of it was fully comprehended.

So, how does grace accomplish this? The grace of God is revealed thus: Christ lived a perfect human life. It was unblemished, unspotted, and unwrinkled by any sin or fault. It is the only human life that has accomplished this. He was perfect in every respect. His thought-life was perfect. His attitudes were perfect. His morals were above reproach. His relationships with others were untarnished in any way. No part of His life offended God. He was the Son of God. After His ascension to Heaven, and His life viewed by the Father, it was obvious to Him that the life of Jesus was 100 percent perfect.

However, Jesus *never* lived His life for Himself. He lived it for others—for *us*. He then proceeded to "impute" this perfect righteousness to anyone who trusts in Him for salvation.

Today, Christ's great gift is His own righteousness. We become right before God not by our rightness, but by Christ's. It is His gift to us. It gains us admission to Heaven and eternity with God. The perfect life of Jesus Christ is given to us and deposited, as it were, into our "bank account" in Heaven. It is now regarded as our own. God regards us as perfectly righteous, acquitted of all guilt and completely justified before Him. God's own righteousness is imputed to us as becoming our own:

> …*It* [righteousness] *shall be imputed to us who believe in Him who raised up Jesus our Lord from the dead* (Rom. 4:24).

By this imputed righteousness through Christ, we are able to stand before God with the same standing as Jesus Himself.

As Job asked, "How should a man be righteous before God?" we may also ask, "How does a man or woman *believe* God?" The answer to that question is in Romans 10:6 and 8-10:

> *The righteousness of faith speaks in this way... The word is near you, in your mouth and in your heart (that is the word of faith which we preach); that if you confess with your mouth the Lord Jesus and believe in your heart that God raised Him from the dead you shall be saved. For with the heart man believes unto righteousness and with the mouth confession is made unto salvation.*

Faith Talks

When the heart believes, the mouth speaks. Faith is not only a matter of the heart, it is also a matter of the mouth. In the chapter on repentance, we spoke of the need to confess sins. The confession of faith is a different kind of confession, even though the original word it is taken from is the same. The Greek word is *homologia*, which means "to say the same as."[4] In other words, it means "to agree with God." When we are sinners we agree with God, admit our sins, agree with the conviction in our hearts, and bring all the hidden works of darkness in our lives into the light.

However, after we have passed through that process, we take on a new form of agreeing with God. Now we agree with the Word that declares we are born again, saved, forgiven, justified, sanctified, accepted, and beloved fellow citizens of the household of God. We are instructed by Scripture to "speak" this, not just believe it, think it, imagine it, or hear it, but *speak* it. This confession is half of the salvation process.

Faith Walks

"Faith walks" means that it *takes action,* it converts from a noun to a *verb*. In James 2:17-26, the apostle comes straight to the point, *"Faith without works is dead."*

Faith that lies dormant in the heart or even the mouth is dead. It is not living. It is useless. It will accomplish nothing. Faith must act in order for it to achieve anything at all. Just a casual reading of Hebrews chapter 11 reveals the great feats of the men and women whom Scripture recognizes as those "of faith." If I believe I can slay the giant, I run to do battle with him.

When I was first saved, I was living with a beautiful young lady named Chris. We were unmarried, but had been involved with each other for about three years. As soon as we were saved, we realized that we could no longer live as we were. We chose to marry; and we did, within three weeks. Our conversion to Christ was real. Real enough to take steps that indicated we believed all that had happened to us was as real as God. Faith *acts*. Living our faith becomes a way of life.

Often, actions of faith are based on nothing else than the Word of God. This can seem crazy to the people around us. However, this is the way of the Kingdom of God. Right at the beginning we make the choice to live by God's ways and not this world's.

3. SONSHIP

How do we become children of God? Two ways!

- First, we are born of God.

- Second, we are adopted by God.

The Lord wants to make utterly sure we are His, and part of the forever family. He does this through both regeneration and adoption.

Regeneration

We have already covered forgiveness and justification. Now let's talk about *regeneration*. Regeneration is being "born again." When we receive Christ we are born again:

> …*unless one is born again, he cannot see the kingdom of God. …unless one is born of water and the Spirit he cannot enter the kingdom of God. That which is born of the flesh is flesh and that which is born of the Spirit is spirit. Do not marvel that I said to you, "you must be born again"* (John 3:3,5-7).

When we are "born again" we become children of God by birth; His Spirit "births" us into the Kingdom. Our entire nature is changed (though we are still "babes" when we first enter the Kingdom). This means we no longer "attempt" to live as God wants us to. It becomes natural to us to be loving, forgiving, joyful. These qualities are ours by way of birthright. We receive these qualities because we are literally "born of the Father" in Heaven. This means the character and nature of God are now imprinted into our lives and we bear the likeness and image of God. This regeneration is obviously an enormous part of our salvation package: …*He saved us, through the washing of regeneration and renewing of the Holy Spirit* (Titus 3:5).

The Holy Spirit is the agent of the new birth.[5] When we are saved, the Father, the Son, and the Holy Spirit come to make us their dwelling place.

Some groups claim that we must be baptized in the Holy Spirit to be saved. This is untrue. Speaking in tongues is a sign of being baptized in the Holy Spirit; however, nowhere in Scripture is there adequate basis for the belief that one has to be baptized in the Holy Spirit and speak in tongues to be saved.

On the other hand, some claim that because we receive the Holy Spirit at the point of the new birth, there is no need to receive the Spirit at a separate and subsequent stage. That also is untrue. We know this because in Luke 24:49 when the disciples were told by Jesus to wait in the city of Jerusalem for the promise of the Father, when they would then be *"endued with power from on high"* (which is the Baptism in the Holy Spirit), they had been saved previously—they had *already* confessed Christ with their mouths and believed in their hearts that He is the Son of God. It was only after Jesus had risen from the grave and appeared to them in John 20:22 that He then "breathed on" them and said to them, *"receive the Holy Spirit."*[5]

When we reach out in faith and ask Christ into our lives, we are then "born" of the Holy Spirit into the Kingdom family of God:

> *But as many as received Him, to them He gave the right to become children of God, to those who believe in His name; who were born, not of blood, nor of the will of the flesh, nor of the will of man, but of God* (John 1:12-13).

Adoption

Becoming a member of God's family means I am adopted by God Himself. The entire reason Jesus came was to *"redeem those who were under the law, that we might receive the adoption as sons"* (Gal. 4:5).

Adoption was the legal route by which a Roman could make a slave a family member. Additionally, if the price of citizenship was paid, the adopted person could also become a Roman citizen. This entitled him to the many privileges that non-Romans did not enjoy.

Adoption also means I am chosen. The parent chooses the child rather than having no choice in the matter. The biological parent has to take "whosoever" arrives; whereas, those adopted are handpicked.

In apostle Paul's mind, the most immediate thought that follows from adoption and sonship is *inheritance*. He consistently points out that because we are God's children, we are also His heirs. Whether adopted or born (in the believer's case, both) we become heirs of God, as Paul explains in Galatians 4:7 and Romans 8:17, *"Therefore you are no longer a slave but a son, and if a son, then an heir of God through Christ"; "...and if children, then heirs—heirs of God and joint heirs with Christ..."* What an amazing statement! All that Christ has inherited from the Father, we have also become entitled to. We are joint heirs with Jesus, who, according to Hebrews 1:2, God appointed as heir of *all things*. There is **nothing** that Christ has not inherited.

This is very relevant to the fact that God has made us His children. On this basis we have become heirs—now in this life and in the one to come—of all things, because we are joint inheritors with Jesus Christ of all that the Father possesses. And that's *everything!*

4. SANCTIFICATION

...But you were washed, but you were sanctified, but you were justified in the name of the Lord Jesus and by the Spirit of our God (1 Corinthians 6:11).

When we receive Christ, He sanctifies us, He makes us holy. Some people think that they need to *become* holy to get saved. Wrong! We get saved to get holy. As mentioned previously, a fish isn't gutted and cleaned before it's caught. When we receive Christ, He goes to work on cleansing us.

> *...you are in Christ Jesus, who became for us...righteousness and sanctification and redemption* (1 Corinthians 1:30).

The Greek word for *sanctification* is the same word that is used for *holy*. It comes from the root word *hagios*, which is used to describe consecration, sacredness, purity, and holiness. It is also translated as "to set apart."[7] To sanctify something is to make it holy, to set it apart for sacred use.

When you are saved, God sanctifies you. He sets you apart for His exclusive use. You are consecrated to Him. Paul tells the Roman Christians to yield to this truth and actively give themselves wholly to God in a "sanctified" lifestyle:

> *"I beseech you therefore, brethren, by the mercies of God, that you present your bodies a living sacrifice, holy, acceptable to God, which is your reasonable service"* (Romans 12:1).

Throughout the New Testament, believers are referred to as "saints." The tradition of "canonizing" certain people after they die, thus making them a saint, is a religious activity without support from Scripture. However, God has no difficulty in calling those who are His and are still alive, "saints" (see Phil. 4:21). This is because He has "made" them so. By the act of the Holy Spirit coming upon us, we are sanctified. In the Old Testament, priests, prophets, kings, people, temples, sacred clothing, and instruments were all anointed with oil when they were set apart for God. They were thus considered "holy." In the New Testament, the oil is the Holy Spirit. When we are born again by the Holy Spirit, He comes to dwell in us. He sanctifies us. The impact of this is that we immediately reject the spirit of the world from our life. A love for purity, holiness, and the presence of God fills our hearts. This is the fruit of sanctification.

5. REDEMPTION

> *In Him we have redemption through His blood...* (Ephesians 1:7).

The Greek word for *redemption* is *apolutrosis*, which means to "buy back" or to "ransom." Another Greek Word for redemption is *lutron*. This word carries the meaning of "something to loosen with, such as a redemption price."[8] The picture is a slave in the slave market having his freedom purchased by someone else. He is "loosed" by his price being paid by another.

Even more, if the slave being sold was actually the son of the purchaser, and somehow over the years the son had drifted from home and found himself caught in a crime, unable to pay the fine, he has to sell himself as a slave to get the money. His father then saw his own child bound and standing on the auction block in the marketplace. The law demanded that the price of freeing a slave was the price of a man. The father, who dearly loved his child, was unable to just come and take him home, as the requirement of the law was that he had to pay the price to free his son.

In this same way, God sent His only begotten Son, Jesus Christ, to purchase us out from slavery. We have been bought back by the price Christ paid to free us: His shed blood, His death.

Or picture it like a young boy who builds a model yacht. He takes it to the river and sails it. A gust of wind catches the little boat and it sails off with the current, moving too fast for the lad to keep up. Finally it disappears in the distance. The boy searches for it day after day with no success. His boat has been lost. Some time later he is in a distant town and comes across a pawn shop. Looking through the window he sees his lost yacht. He goes to the counter and tells the owner that he is the owner of the boat in the window. The shop keeper tells him he is wrong. He is the owner now because someone sold it to him. The boy asks how he can recover the boat. The answer is obvious: purchase it. The boy finds the money, pays the man, and walks away with the boat he has redeemed. It is something he has "bought back."

The powerful idea that flows from this story is that we are now the possession of God, purchased back to Him by the price of the blood of Christ. We are His property.

> *...you are not your own? For you were bought at a price; therefore glorify God in your body and in your spirit, which are God's* (1 Corinthians 6:19-20).

Our faith in God will always be strong when it is based on the Word of God, and not just our own thoughts and feelings. These are important to our Christian experience, but they must harmonize with the Word. Our faith will be strong because we realize that we are God's property. We are His responsibility. He has taken it on Himself to ensure that we are well cared for. He has purchased us, redeemed us from the hand of the devil, from the power of sin, and from judgment itself. Our afterlife destination is no longer hell, it is Heaven. We have been forgiven, justified, regenerated, adopted, sanctified, and redeemed. Our admission to Heaven is signed, sealed, and delivered, and comes with the most powerful of assurances: *What*

then shall we say to these things? If God is for us, who can be against us?
(Rom. 8:31)

FAITH IN WHAT?

We know that the Holy Spirit is invisible, that we fellowship with the Spirit by faith not by sight, and that we walk with the Spirit by faith. Thus, faith lives by the invisible world, and believers walk by that faith (that is, not by this visible world). Faith is the foundation upon which we move in the Spirit of God in three different areas: in His Word, in Him, and in ourselves. Let's examine each.

1. Faith in God's Word

If we desire to walk in the Spirit, we must have a firm grasp of the Word of God. The Holy Spirit moves within the boundaries of the Word of God. The Word of God is totally God-breathed (see 2 Tim. 3:16). The Bible is Spirit inspired. The Bible is authored by men under the influence of the Holy Spirit. *The Bible is the tangible **mind** of God.* The Word and the Spirit are in complete harmony. The Spirit agrees with the Word. The Word agrees with the Spirit.

God confirms His Word—not the word of man, but the Word of God (see Mark 16:20). Our faith is in the Word. What the Word says about the Holy Spirit is what the Holy Spirit is revealing about Himself. He unfolds how He operates. John 7:37 (KJV) declares the person believing in Christ has *"out of his belly shall flow rivers of living water"* that is, out of his or her inner spirit. This means the Holy Spirit flows out of me when I act on the Word.

Faith understands that feelings are unreliable as the basis for action. Neither does faith rely on our natural senses. Nor does it rely on past experiences or on the experience of others. It does not rely on others' opinion. It does not depend on our ability. Faith relies on one thing: *What God has said—His Word!*

Your word is a lamp to my feet and a light to my path (Ps. 119:105). This means I take steps based on the Word of God. Initially, I have no physical evidence of what I am believing. I doubt I will ever see a literal river flowing from my inner self. However, I definitely believe the Holy Spirit is pouring out of my life into others as I preach. When we're counseling someone, the Holy Ghost flows from us to that person. When I worship, the Spirit of God is flowing out of me into the heavens as a river of inspired praise to God. When I pray or prophesy over someone, the Holy Spirit is pouring into that person's life. How do I know this is so? Not by the sight of my eyes. Not by my feelings. I am assured by the infallible Word of God. That's how it is!!

Other Scriptures also point to this. As we believe God's Word and act on it, the truth we believe becomes reality. It translates from being a principle on paper to reality in this physical world. God moves in response to faith, without which, it is *impossible* to please Him (see Heb. 11:6).

To move in the Holy Spirit is to move in faith. The two are inseparable.

2. Faith in God

To move in the Spirit is also to believe in God's integrity. He is faithful to what He has said. He declared He will work with us confirming His word. Jesus says in Mark 11:22, *"Have faith in God."*

Faith sees God at work *in* us. Faith sees God at work *through* us. You believe as you pray. The power of God brings answers. Faith sees answers before they happen. Fear sees failure and despair. Both faith and fear use the imagination. Fear comes naturally to the human heart. Faith does not. We must make the decision to believe. By this decision, doubt is displaced—by faith. *Let not your heart be troubled; you believe in God, believe also in Me* (John 14:1).

This means we can make the choice to not be anxious. Equally important is that we can decide what to believe. *For God has not given us a spirit of fear, but of power and of love and of a sound mind* (2 Tim. 1:7).

Much of what the Word of God says is not visible. This does not mean it is not at work, however, or not real. The Bible is truth. We walk by truth rather than by circumstances. Facts and truth are often very different. The realities of Scripture incarnate as we make the decision to act on the Word of God because of faith living inside us.

3. Faith in Ourselves

Learning to hear God's voice is a lifetime pursuit. His voice is distinct from all the other clamor going on inside us. This "unction" is how we are "led by the Spirit." We discover the voice of God as we spend time with Him. We also discern the voice of God through mistakes and trials.

Uncertainty about the voice of God can be the weakest link in the chain of our potential for moving in the Spirit. People often do not believe that what they are feeling is from God, or that it holds any great significance.

Edward Millar was involved in the 1940s Argentinean revival. I met him in 1973. He told how the revival began. He was a missionary from America to Argentina. The missions board stopped his support when they heard he was no longer distributing tracts but rather spending whole days in prayer. He felt he should convene a prayer meeting. Only a handful of people arrived. Even then he was the only one prepared to pray. One young woman came every night. However, she prayed not one word. Ed attempted to find why God asked him to call the meeting. He asked if anyone "felt" to do anything. The young woman replied she felt like striking the table. She wouldn't do it, however. She said she felt foolish doing something that carried little significance. After three nights (and nothing happening) she was finally persuaded to hit the table. Millar suggested they all walk around the table and strike it, one after another. When the particular woman finally hit it, the room filled with the glory of God. They all spent hours in the presence of the Lord. From that point, a great revival broke out in Argentina with literally hundreds of thousands turning to Christ. During the revival, an enormous number of miracles happened through evangelist Tommy Hicks.

Although a woman hitting a table obviously is not the only element triggering a revival of these proportions, Edward Miller felt her obedience played a part in releasing a move of the Holy Spirit.

Doubt and the Devil

We must have faith in our ability to receive impressions from God. We must be prepared to act on them. Self-doubt is the most insidious weapon satan uses against God's people. This alone most hinders the release of the Spirit.

When the devil tempts Jesus in the wilderness, he begins his taunt with *"if."* Jesus is tempted to doubt He is who God actually says He is. He is tempted to prove to Himself that He actually is the Son of God. But we know He doesn't yield. He doesn't succumb to self-doubt. Rather, He builds His faith and resists satan with the Word of God. As He speaks the Word, His faith increases and the devil is defeated. The two-edged sword works.

The early disciples prayed for boldness to preach the Word. Walking in this confidence they were fully inspired, empowered, and led by the Holy Ghost. This is what they acted on and that is why their success for the Kingdom was so spectacular.

Oral Roberts said he had never seen God use a discouraged man. The Spirit moves through men and women who are bold, confident, and assured. This confidence (faith) is based on the Word of God, and what we hear from God—a *rhema*. This is the source of faith. Sadly, some people have little confidence that it actually is God speaking. We are tempted to pass off the impression as mere imagination. Certainly our imaginations can be overactive, but as we stay filled with the Spirit and spend time communing with Him, we are able to discern between His voice and any others.

Have Faith That It Is God

When we pray for the sick we should be led by the Spirit in timing, pace, words, actions, and the instructions we give. Confidence to act on impressions from the Lord, comes only from doing it.

There may be times when we seem to fail, but many times we will succeed. Hebrews says we become mature by using what God has given us (see Heb. 5:14). We act on impressions from God. It works, and we gain confidence.

We must believe God is communicating with us, through inner impressions, through other people, and the desires and burdens of our hearts, inspirations, circumstances. All that God is looking for is someone who is *attentive.* Someone who *hearkens,* as the King James Version puts it. The Bible constantly repeats this call: *willingness to "hearken" to the Lord* (see Isa. 55:2). This is *hearing* and *doing* what God says.

When the prophet Samuel was just a boy, he heard a voice calling him, but didn't understand that it was God. However, after this occurred three times, his teacher, Eli, recognized this was God. He told the boy to answer with, *"Speak, Lord, for your servant hears"* (1 Sam. 3:9). Samuel does this and receives his first message. He is to pronounce judgment on Eli the high priest and his family. Talk about being thrown into the deep end!

First Kings 19 relates the story of Elijah becoming desperate to hear the voice of God. He journeys for six weeks to Mount Horeb. He ascends the mountain, finding a cave. Soon after arriving, God releases three awesome demonstrations of enormous power. A wind roars with rock-breaking force across the cave's mouth. An earthquake shakes the mountain like a leaf. Fire burns across the mountainside, destroying everything in its path. However, Scripture takes pains to explain that God is in neither the wind, nor the earthquake, nor the fire. Instead, He is in a quiet, still, small voice. And Elijah heard Him.

To hear God's voice, be "still." *Still* means two things. First, we are quiet within. This is difficult unless we spend time in quiet with*out.* Alone, with no noise, in a place where we meet God. People complain they have no such place. I travel to a lot of different places and find myself in hundreds of different circumstances. I have found that where there's a will, there's a way. It may be simply sitting somewhere with my eyes closed, even though I might be in an airport surrounded with people and noise. A quiet place can be found, if we're hungry enough for fellowship with the Lord. I need to pray. I need the Word of God. I need to hear God.

The second aspect of stillness is that we *stop*. We cease going somewhere, anywhere. We wait patiently. As a servant waits for commands from his master, so the servant of God comes before Him with patience—a "waiting" attitude. This is honoring God. It is reverence.

POSITIVE, BOLD PATIENCE

Many of the trials we face are designed to develop patience. This trait is a powerful characteristic for believers. It supplies staying power in the presence of God. When we begin to pray, we think of a thousand and one things we could be otherwise doing. Even when we are breaking through into the presence of God, tremendous urges to do other things arise. Patience holds us in His presence until we receive all God has for us. This quality calms the soul. We learn to wait upon the Lord.

God is waiting for His people to wait for Him! Faith pleases God!

Sincerity is too weak on its own to live life successfully. Add faith to your sincerity.

We hope in vain if we hope that sincerity alone will please God. "At least I'm sincere!" doesn't atone for a fearful life. It is actually bold, confident faith in a true heart that gains God's favor.

Sincerity must walk together with confidence.

Sure, you're sincere, but on its own does it achieve the things you are looking for?

Sure, you sincerely believe this and that, but does it achieve results?

God tells Joshua to be bold, be strong, and be very courageous. These are the great character traits of those who possess their Promised Land.

Step out in boldness. Be bold, be confident! Go the bold!

A Christian without courage is a Christian without power. Amazingly, courage can even prevail over wisdom. Think of David versus Goliath. The strong persist through discouragement. They pursue even when their heart flags.

Develop relationships with encouraging people. Remove unnecessary discouraging influences from your life. Let everything that you are involved in build you up. Watch, read, and listen to what builds you up. God moves through people of courage.

HAVE FAITH!

Good leaders hold a positive view of the future. We believe God fulfills our dreams.

Our desires exceed what we have and where we are. We ask God to hear our prayers.

We build our faith through reading, meditating, studying, and speaking the incredible promises of God.

Vision is the gift of faith in action. Leadership is clear vision. A leader is bold and sees the future. *He who believes in Me, as the Scripture has said, out of his heart will flow rivers of living water* (John 7:38).

A basic law of life is this: what lives, grows. Churches that are dead do not grow. Dead products go nowhere. Recognize what's dead and bury it. Don't allow politics, loyalties, or sentiments to hijack your resources to attempt keeping a dead thing alive. If the horse is dead, dismount! People are attracted to life! Create life all around you. Be bright and life-giving. People want this more than they want money. If it's alive, it'll grow. Basic!

> *No pessimist ever discovered the secret of the stars, or sailed to an uncharted land, or opened a new doorway for the human spirit.* —Helen Keller

The human nature veers toward the negative without any help at all.

If you want to grow weeds in your garden, do nothing with the garden. If you want to grow good plants, that takes effort. It means removing weeds regularly.

Constant vigilance keeps our minds and hearts free from the negative.

Our minds are like soil. Plant potatoes, reap potatoes. Plant roses, reap roses.

Faith or no faith? Positive or negative? The choice is yours. To the faithless, negative easily hijacks our focus. It takes no effort at all to be negative, and it pleases no one. It takes effort to have faith, and it pleases God.

We will discuss faith as a spiritual gift in Foundation Four.

ENDNOTES

1. Robert Young, *Young's Analytical Concordance to the Bible* (Hendrickson, 1984).

2. *Strong's Dictionary,* #G1344.

3. *Strong's Dictionary,* #H6665.

4. *Strong's Dictionary,* #G3671.

5. Regeneration is not the Baptism of the Holy Spirit, which will be addressed in Foundation Three.

6. Jesus telling the disciples after they'd been saved that they would *later* be endued with "power from on high" and then later said to them "receive the Holy Spirit," displays that *baptizing in* the Holy Spirit is different from *receiving* the Holy Spirit at the moment of believing, confessing, and accepting Christ as Savior.

7. *Strong's Dictionary*, #G40.

8. *Strong's Dictionary*, #G3083.

—

Baptisms

BAPTISM LITERALLY MEANS **"TO IMMERSE INTO."** Jesus commands us to be baptized as part of choosing to follow Him. We are to be baptized in:

1. Water

2. The Holy Spirit

3. The Church

4. Fire

Baptism is a word that tells us we are to be totally immersed. The real Christian life is a 100 percent commitment. It is impossible to live this life any other way. Thus, we must be baptized into those elements that will empower us to live the most magnificent life on earth.

ORIGIN OF THE WORD *BAPTISM*

The word *baptism* is an Anglicized word. This means that when it was translated into the English language from the Greek, it was basically left as it was. There were reasons surrounding this. Way back when the Pope, head of the early church based in Rome, refused to grant King Henry VIII a divorce, Henry decided that he would nationalize the church in England and break away from the church based in Rome. Thus began the Church of England.

Fast forward to the time of King James I of England. As the recognized head of the Church of England, when he commissioned the Bible to be translated from Greek into English, he instructed them to leave certain Bible transliterations as they were. The Greek word for the term "to baptize" is *bapto*, which means "to whelm...to cover wholly with a fluid...to make fully wet."[1] Thus, in the early church, people were baptized by *full immersion* into the water. However, as time went by, for one reason or another, the practice of plunging new believers beneath the water passed away.

Other important first-century church teachings were also dispensed with, such as carrying out the baptism ceremony only when the believer was of an age and understanding of what he was doing. Babies were baptized as a matter of religious practice solely on the basis of whether the parents were members of the church. Eventually, a person's spiritual state no longer seemed to matter to the church; the "ceremony" was sufficient. The practice of baptism then became a ritual of merely sprinkling with water, and one was admitted to the church. However, the custom then began to be seen as the process whereby the person became acceptable to God. Thus, a person was thought to become a Christian simply by virtue of his having been baptized as an infant.

This has always been the danger of religious "acts." Too easily they can degenerate to heartless, empty, lip-serving traditions. These are, at best, false securities. At worst, they are vigorous enemies against God, and all the work of Jesus and the apostles.

In his *Foundation Series*, Derek Prince writes:

> The relationship between James I and his bishops was not always too cordial and he did not wish the new translation of the Bible, published in his name and with his authority, to make his relationship with the bishops any worse. For this reason he allowed it to be understood that as far as possible, nothing was to be introduced into the translation which would cause unnecessary offense to the bishops or which would be too obviously contrary to the practices of the established church. Hence, the Greek word baptizo, which could easily have become, in translation, a source of controversy, was never translated at all, but was simply written over in the English language.

> Bapto is related to washings and ablutions of all kinds. It is important that we understand the full meaning of this word, because it relates to areas other than just water baptism. There is the Baptism in the Holy Spirit, the Baptism into Christ's Body, and the Baptism of Suffering; and none of these refer to a sprinkling of the experience. They all refer to a *complete immersion.*[2]

If we allow ourselves to think that baptism is ceremonial, participated in without any intelligent understanding of the event, and simply a sprinkling, then we dilute God's work in people's lives to an almost nonexistent level. Sadly, this is exactly the case in much of traditional Christianity.

RECOVERY OF FULL IMMERSION

In 1608, John Smyth baptized himself in Amsterdam. This was basically the beginning of the Baptist movement as we know it today. This group recovered the vital truth of adult, full immersion as a fulfillment of Christ's command to "be baptized."

Baptism as practiced by Christians in the New Testament has its roots in the very beginning of the Old Testament. The great flood of Genesis chapter 7 is a symbol of water baptism in that the entire old generation perished in the water except for Noah, his wife, his three sons and their wives; and the new generation was saved, thus beginning a whole new world, as noted by Peter:

> *...once the Divine longsuffering waited in the days of Noah, while the ark was being prepared, in which a few, that is, eight souls, were saved through water. There is also an antitype which now saves us—baptism...* (1 Peter 3:20-21).

Another picture showing deliverance from the old as we enter the new is the Exodus 14 account of Moses crossing the Red Sea with three million Hebrews behind him, as noted by Paul:

> *...all our fathers were under the cloud, all passed through the sea, all were baptized into Moses in the cloud and in the sea* (1 Corinthians 10:1-2).

These two images are taken from events in the Old Testament. However, as a practice, baptism actually has its beginnings in the Tabernacle of Moses: the priests were required to cleanse themselves regularly in a large bowl called the laver, which was positioned immediately after the great bronze altar between the tabernacle of the congregation and the altar used for burnt sacrifices to God (see Exod. 30:18). The laver itself had been made from the donated bronze mirrors of the Israelite women. Parts of the sacrificial animals were also washed in the laver. The concept of cleansing by water as part of our approach to God was thus introduced.

NAAMAN

The next event that prepared the way for baptism is found in Second Kings 5. It is the story of Naaman, a commander of the army of the king of Syria. Although Naaman is a famous warrior with a powerful position in his nation, he is also a leper. One of the foreign maids he had abducted from Israel advises him that there is a cure to be found for him in her country. She knows that the prophet Elisha can heal Naaman of his leprosy. The commander makes the journey to the prophet, whose instructions are that the great Naaman must dip himself seven times in the River Jordan if he is to be healed. Although he initially resists the command, he eventually carries it out and is completely healed of leprosy.

Leprosy is always seen as a symbol of sin in the Old Testament. This lucidly sets the stage for John the Baptist at the River Jordan.

JOHN THE BAPTIST

In the Book of John (and in Mark 1 and Matthew 3), the Baptist is found in the desert preaching a message of repentance to the Israelites. Those who wish to act on what he is calling for must make a public profession that they are in fact leaving sin and turning to righteousness. The sign of their intent is that they are baptized, fully immersed as adults, in the River Jordan. It was an outward expression of an internal change of heart.

The Bible tells us that the whole region went out to John. He was experiencing a vast move of God. John knew his purpose—to prepare the way for another: Jesus. John's cousin Jesus arrives in the middle of this revival and asks John to baptize Him too. Even though He has no sin, He says it is necessary to do this in order to *"fulfill all righteousness"* (Matt. 3:15).

CHRIST: OUR PATTERN

If Christ without sin sought to be baptized in water, it behooves us who need to indicate our cleansing from sin to *do the same*. Scripture makes it clear: Jesus was baptized by full immersion into the water. We know this because after He had been baptized, as stated in Matthew 3:16, *"He came up immediately from the water."* Jesus is our "pattern Man." He established the path, as Peter said, *"leaving us an example that you should follow His steps"* (1 Pet. 2:21).

Interestingly enough, Jesus Himself begins to minister almost immediately after this. He first spends forty days away in the desert, fasting. After which, He begins his ministry. He preaches exactly the same message that John preached, and He also begins baptizing: *From that time Jesus began to preach and to say, "Repent, for the kingdom of Heaven is at hand"* (Matt. 4:17).

> *And they came to John and said to him, "Rabbi, He who was with you beyond Jordan, to whom you have testified—behold, He is baptizing and all are coming to Him!* (John 3:26)

Piggybacking

It is fascinating that the Son of God did not immediately establish

His uniqueness by completely discarding his forerunner's message and proclaiming His ministry. Here is a lesson for all of us: Christ "piggybacked" into ministry. He did not see "originality" as necessary for Him to be credible. From the start, Jesus preached exactly the same message as John the Baptist. He also continued the practice of baptizing. His entry to the ministry was sponsored and endorsed by the one who obviously was the man of the moment: John.

Some young upstarts today have not felt the need for this endorsement, thinking that their particular unique ministry will establish itself all on its own. *Wrong*. We all need someone to open the door in the early days. We are foolish to depart from something that is obviously working, simply because we are too proud to appear to be copying another.

Jesus also realized that the people John had "prepared" were destined to follow Him. He knew that if change was to take place it must be gentle and not sudden. Thus, those whom John had prepared for Christ found the transition from John to Jesus untroubled by challenges to what they had previously accepted as the way God was moving.

NEW TESTAMENT CHRISTIANS

After Christ had risen from the dead and the Holy Spirit fell, baptism did not lose any of its significance. It continued as the recognized manner in which people would publicly declare their commitment to repent and turn to God. Believers were quickly baptized after conversion: *Then those who gladly received his word were baptized...* (Acts 2:41). *...And immediately he and all his family were baptized...* (Acts 16:33).

Additionally, not only did water baptism continue as an accepted practice of the church, its importance ascended to being an accompanying act to salvation: *He who believes and is baptized will be saved; but he who does not believe will be condemned* (Mark 16:16).

BAPTISM MEANS DEATH

Baptism gained further significance in the walk of the believer. Paul proclaims his revelation of the victory the believer gains through water baptism. Essentially, when we were saved, not only were our sins forgiven, but the sins of the person who committed those offenses (the sinner) were also blotted out. It is obvious that simply plucking the fruit from a tree, no matter how sour it may be, will not prevent the tree from continuing to yield that same bad fruit. The tree itself must be killed. However, to "do away" with the believer after he has chosen Christ is obviously not going to work. Yet, it was definitely God's will to accomplish that, because the nature of humankind has a bias toward sin, which arrives the day we are conceived: *Behold, I was brought forth in iniquity, and in sin my mother conceived me* (Ps. 51:5).

Sin is evidenced very early in our career on earth. A child rarely needs instruction on how to do wrong. All our teaching focuses on how to live right. We spend large amounts of time correcting our children as they grow, with commandments and teachings, penalties and punishments. All of us—male and female—inherited this sinful nature from Adam and Eve, the original sinners, our original parents. It is called the "flesh," "the old man," "the body of sin," "the carnal man," "the Adamic nature." It is this nature, Paul declares, that must be destroyed.

Baptism in water is our statement that not only are we turning from sin, but we are also dying to it. We are declaring that the entirety of our old life and the entirety of our sinful nature are now dead. We are also saying that we are being resurrected into a totally new life in Christ. Being lowered into the waters of baptism is being crucified and buried with Christ. Being lifted up out of the water is being resurrected with Christ. Baptism is God's means of identifying us with the death, burial, and resurrection of Jesus Christ.

> *Or do you not know that as many of us as were baptized into Christ Jesus were baptized into his death? Therefore we were buried with Him through baptism into death, that just as Christ was raised from the dead by the glory of the Father, even so we should walk in newness of life. For if we have been united together in the likeness of his death, certainly we shall also be in the likeness of His resurrection* (Romans 6:3-5).

FAITH MAKES TRUTH REAL

The key to truth becoming real is *faith*. Faith "reckons" the truth to be activated. The day we are baptized, a life dies. Our old sinful nature dies. A new nature is born. This nature is in the image of Christ. It has a bias toward righteousness. It wants to do the right thing. The struggle we had with sin finishes as we take this Scripture and embrace it as being our own.

BAPTISM OF THE HOLY SPIRIT

Just like the baptism in water, the Baptism of the Holy Spirit is a totally "immersed" experience—we are not "sprinkled" with the Holy Spirit. Also as with baptism in water, Baptism of the Holy Spirit is intended for every believer: *For the promise is to you and to your children, and to all who are afar off, as many as the Lord our God will call* (Acts 2:39).

Jesus told His disciples not to depart from Jerusalem but to wait until they received the *"Promise of the Father"* (Acts 1:4). It was as though He was saying to them, "Go into all the world and *preach*, but don't *do* anything for Me until you have the same power that I received at the Jordan. You need the Holy Spirit just like I needed Him. Don't think you can represent Me without the power of God."

Sadly, for much of our history we have ignored the command of Jesus to wait for the promise of the Father (which was that we would be baptized with the Holy Spirit), and attempt to do the works of Christ in our own ability. However, in our own power, we will never represent Christ properly. He operated in a supernatural power and He never authorized any of us to do ministry any differently. If Jesus saw that He, the Son of God was in need of the power of the Spirit, then we are too...

Happily, since the turn of the last century, there has been an amazing outpouring of the Holy Spirit and an ever-increasing acceptance of this experience in the church.[3] More and more Christians, tired of empty ceremony, are hungry to experience God.

POWER FROM ON HIGH

Behold I send the Promise of My Father upon you; but tarry in the city of Jerusalem until you are endued with power from on high (Luke 24:49).

The word *endued* means "clothed." This is "power clothing" for serving Christ. It is not for salvation (that comes through faith in

Christ, receiving the forgiveness of sins and being born again by the Holy Spirit). The Baptism of the Holy Spirit is *separate from* and *subsequent to* the work of salvation.

Most definitely the Holy Spirit comes to dwell within us at the point of the new birth:

> *Or do you not know that your body is the temple of the Holy Spirit who is in you, whom you have from God, and you are not your own?* (1 Corinthians 6:19)

If anyone does not have the Spirit of Christ, he does not belong to Christ (Rom. 8:9 NIV). But *empowerment for service* is another matter. The Baptism of the Holy Spirit is not for salvation, but for service—supernatural service. The kind that Christ brought to this world.

POWER

The word translated as "power" comes from the Greek word *dunamis*, which is the root of our words *dynamo* and *dynamite*.[4] Christ intended this to be a powerful experience. Part of the reason Christianity has been widely regarded as a weak and powerless religion is because it has been exactly that. It takes the Baptism of the Holy Spirit to put the dynamite back into the Church, so it is like dynamite in society.

THE PENTECOSTAL POSITION

The New Testament abounds with acts of the Holy Spirit. Paul gives the most thorough teaching of this in the Book of First Corinthians. In the Book of Acts, the "baptizing of the Spirit" is recorded as happening five times. In these teachings and examples, we find a consistent thread running throughout: the experience was always evidenced by a *supernatural manifestation*. Most often it is identified as "speaking in tongues."

The Pentecostals have held to the fact that the "initial evidence" of the baptism in the Holy Spirit is, in fact, speaking in tongues. They have held to this at the expense of rejection and persecutions of all kinds in times past. Yet, this has returned power to the Church simply because these guardians of truth would not allow it to be compromised.

Tongues is called "the least of the gifts." This being true, God has lowered the entrance point for us into the supernatural world to the least level of difficulty. Even still, many oppose this. They say there are other evidences of the Baptism of the Holy Spirit. This is difficult to support from Scripture. Often arguments of this kind are only to make life more comfortable for those who take issue with speaking in tongues. However, we shouldn't be found forcing Scripture to accommodate our experience or lack of it. Why should we let ourselves be robbed of what God has for us, simply because of pride or fear?

Some have even been taught by their particular denomination that tongues is actually from the devil.[5] Sadly, there are still barriers to overcome for this Baptism to become a reality in the life of the Body of Christ worldwide.

MY EXPERIENCE

I was converted twenty-five years ago. I had been a member of the "drop out generation." Feeling the emptiness of the materialistic world, I was on a heady search for truth. This led me down all sorts of paths, including "mind-expanding" drugs and occult involvements.

Anything spiritual was not regarded as witchcraft, but really as part of searching. However, I didn't escape the effects of fooling with the devil. A deep fear clouded my mind. Sleeping was difficult. I would awake with horrifying visions of devils. I sought out the address of a spiritualist group known to a friend of mine. But her mother had been born again just two weeks before, so she told her daughter to tell me to go to her church instead.

I had no knowledge of God whatsoever—*none!* I didn't even realize that God and Jesus were related! I didn't realize that God and the Bible went together. Any Bible knowledge I had received as a child was long lost. I walked into this little Pentecostal church and was struck dumb. The power of God came upon me and stayed on me through the entire service. I was simply stunned. I went forward at the end to receive Christ. They took me out to a back room to be prayed for.

Some old men, called elders, came to pray for me. They laid hands on me and began rebuking the devil. I felt a strange black cloud surface in my emotions. I began to cry. The cloud rose up within me and eventually lifted right off the top of my head. I was really weeping by then. My hands were lifted up in the air. I felt a strange language come into my mouth. I was vaguely aware that the elders around me were also speaking in some odd speech. It was as though someone inside me nodded and said, "Go ahead." I began to speak in this strange but beautiful language. After all this, I hugged all the elders. I was full of a love I had never felt before.

It seems amazing to me that without any teaching at all on the subject, the Spirit found a way into my life and transformed it in one great day. These people believed that when people are baptized in the Holy Spirit, they would speak in tongues.

While Peter was still speaking these words, the Holy Spirit came on all who heard the message. The circumcised believers who had come with Peter were astonished that the gift of the Holy Spirit had been poured out even on the Gentiles. For they heard them speaking in tongues and praising God (Acts 10:44-46 NIV).

TONGUES: EVIDENCE OF THE BAPTISM OF THE HOLY SPIRIT

Down through history this fact of tongues indicating the presence of the Holy Spirit has been evidenced in the Church as the norm.

The following quotes are taken from the book *Which Bible Can We Trust?* by Les Garrett:

- A.D. **150, Justin Martyr:** "Come into our assemblies and there you will see Him (The Holy Spirit) cast out demons, heal the sick, hear Him speak in tongues."

- A.D. **300, Chrysostom of Constantinople:** "Whoever was baptized in Apostolic days, straightway spoke with tongues."

- A.D. **400, Augustine, Bishop of Hippo:** "We still do what the Apostles did when they laid hands on the Samaritans and called down the Holy Spirit on them in the laying on of hands. It is expected that converts should speak with new tongues."

- A.D. **1520, Martin Luther:** "Dr. Martin Luther was a prophet, evangelist, speaker in tongues and interpreter in one person, endowed with all the gifts of the Spirit."

- A.D. **1750, Thomas Walsh:** In the diary of Thomas Walsh, one of Wesley's foremost preachers, dated the 8th of March, 1750, the record stands: "This morning the Lord gave me a language that I knew not of, raising my soul to Him in a wonderful manner."

- A.D. **1882, Dwight L. Moody:** "When I, a YMCA member, got to the rooms of the Young Men's Christian Association (Victoria Hall London) I found the meeting 'on fire.' The young men were speaking with tongues, prophesying. What on earth did it mean? Only that Moody had been addressing them that afternoon!"

Many other descriptions of great historical figures such as Charles Finney, General William Booth, Charles Spurgeon, and others abound with experiences of the Baptism of the Holy Spirit, accompanied with manifestations such as speaking in tongues.

The Bible prophesies it, records its happening, and teaches on it. The prophet Joel even prophesies the event as being a sign of the "last days":

And it shall come to pass afterward that I will pour out My Spirit on all flesh; your sons and your daughters shall prophesy, your old men shall dream dreams, your young men shall see visions (Joel 2:28).

In Isaiah 28 when the leaders ridiculed Isaiah's prophecies as gibberish and respond to him as if he is talking down to them, Isaiah responds by warning them that God will judge them through Assyrian invaders speaking in another tongue: *"For with stammering lips and another tongue He will speak to this people"* (Isa. 28:11). In First Corinthians 14:21, apostle Paul uses this as an example that one of the uses of the New Testament gift of tongues and interpretation of tongues is as a warning to unbelievers.

We will discuss in more detail Tongues and Interpretation of Tongues in the next Foundation chapter titled Spiritual Gifts.

FIVE EXAMPLES: BAPTISM OF THE HOLY SPIRIT

1. The Day of Pentecost

The historical record of the Book of Acts gives five examples of people receiving the Baptism of the Holy Spirit. In each case the people are found speaking in tongues. The first example takes place on the Day of Pentecost:

And they were all filled with the Holy Spirit and began to speak with other tongues, as the Spirit gave them utterance (Acts 2:4).

We cannot afford to reduce it merely to an emotional experience of joy, but the disciples were filled *"with great joy"* when they returned to Jerusalem (Luke 24:52). The apostles had been faithful to the command of Christ not to depart from Jerusalem. They were on their way to receive the Baptism and they were filled with joy because they had the promise of it from Jesus (see Luke 24:49). They waited and waited, not even knowing what was in store for them. On the day of Pentecost, it fell. All Heaven broke loose on that first gathering of Christ's followers as the Church. This was the birthing of the mighty Church of God.

AN OLD TESTAMENT FORESHADOWING

A fantastic synchronicity of events occurs here. When Israel was delivered from Egyptian bondage, the final "wonder" that God performed was when He sent an "angel of death" throughout the land and took all the firstborn. He instructed every Israelite to slay a lamb and to sprinkle the blood of the sacrifice over the doorposts at the front of the house. When the angel of death saw the blood, it would "pass over" that home and no death would occur. (See Exodus 12:12-14.)

Then Israel makes its exodus from Egypt into the desert. Finally, they arrive at the base of Mount Sinai. God summons Moses to ascend the Mount. The man of God disappears up into a fiery cloud at the peak and remains there for forty days. During this time, God delivers instructions to Moses for this "people of God." They are to become a nation of their own. Moses is to lead them to a tract of land God has prepared for them. The requirements of God are made clear to Moses, who is to be the lawgiver for the nation. The ten most important commands are written on two tablets of stone with the finger of God. The Decalogue (Ten Commandments) is what Moses brought down from the mountain. (See Exodus 24:12-18.)

Exodus 32 tells the story of when Moses arrived back at the base of Mount Sinai and found the people had already backslidden. They had made a false god, they were involved in a wild sexual orgy, and they all were complaining about their current circumstances and wanted to return to Egypt. The anger of God arose in Moses. He destroyed the two tablets and called for all those who did not wish to give total allegiance to Yahweh to stand to one side. Three thousand did, and the man of God commanded that they be slain on the spot.

The giving of the law was celebrated in the history of Israel as Pentecost. Jewish rabbis taught that the law was given fifty days after Passover (the Greek word *pentekoste* means the fiftieth day). This celebration was also a feast that acknowledged the ingathering of crops and their dedication to God. It was also called the "Feast of Weeks" (see Exod. 34:22), "Feast of Harvest" (see Exod. 23:16), and "Day of First Fruits" (see Num. 28:26).

After Jesus rose from the dead, He appeared to His disciples over a period of approximately forty days. The disciples then went to Jerusalem and waited for another ten days. On the tenth day, the exact day of Pentecost—the fiftieth day since Jesus had risen from the grave—the Holy Spirit fell.

We travel through our lives dealing with circumstances we find ourselves in, mostly unconscious of anything at all influencing our steps. Yet, here is one (of many) incredible examples of God keeping time with His program. His sovereign hand oversees and directs the steps of His children, conforming them to a plan that He laid down since the beginning of time.

Our "heavenly Moses," Jesus, ascended the "hill of the Lord" and obtained a new law for us, a New Testament in which the Spirit is the law by which we live. Long before then, the prophet Ezekiel foresaw that day:

> *I will put My Spirit within you and cause you to walk in My statutes, and you will keep My judgments and do them* (Ezekiel 36:27).

THE LAW OF THE SPIRIT OF LIFE

Paul also recognizes that a new law has been given—and in a totally different manner. Under the Old Testament, the requirements were on the outside, on two tablets of stone. In the New Testament, the Law is inscribed on the heart (it is "felt" within). Not only that, but the desire to fulfill the requirements (that is, to be righteous) is also placed in the heart. As we have seen in the study on water baptism, the flesh had no power to be righteous. Rather the opposite. The flesh has a bias toward wrong. In the New Testament, we are empowered to do the right thing by the presence of the Holy Spirit:

> *Clearly you are an epistle of Christ, ministered by us, written not with ink but written by the Spirit of the living God, not on tablets of stone, but on tablets of flesh, that is, of the heart* (2 Corinthians 3:3).

NEW TONGUES

When the Spirit initially fell, the disciples spoke with "other" tongues. Let me talk about this for a moment: Jesus tells His followers in Mark 16:17 that those who believe on Him will, among other things, *"speak with new tongues."* Thus we have a heading: *New Tongues.* Under this heading there are three different expressions of the gift: Other Tongues, Unknown Tongues, and Angelic Tongues:

OTHER TONGUES

This is when the Spirit empowers a person to speak a foreign language that they have not learned. The speaker supernaturally communicates a message from the Lord in another language to people. Obviously, it is the language of the hearers. This is what happened on the day of Pentecost. Many foreign proselytes were attending the Feasts of Passover and Pentecost. God wanted to speak to them. He did so in their own languages, through the newly Spirit-filled disciples. This is people speaking to people supernaturally.

UNKNOWN TONGUES

In First Corinthians 14:2 Paul says, *"He who speaks in a* [unknown] *tongue does not speak to men but to God, for no one understands him; however, in the Spirit he speaks mysteries."* This means that the language here is different from that on the Day of Pentecost. No one understands this language. Today, this is sometimes referred to as *glossolalia.* The gift of new tongues is most often expressed like this. Although unintelligible to others, it is intelligible to God. This is us speaking to God supernaturally. Speaking in unknown tongues, the believer *"edifies himself."* Paul commands us to *"forbid not"* speaking in tongues (see 1 Cor. 14:39).

ANGELIC TONGUES

This is when God speaks to us supernaturally. When we get together as the Church, the gifts of the Spirit are often manifested. One of those gifts can be a message in tongues. This generally comes in the worship or prayer time. It comes with an authority and a sense of import that exceeds the general worship time.

The Corinthian church was suffering the problem of overzealous Christians all wanting to bring their "message." They would voice their messages in tongues or prophecies all at the same time, without waiting for one another. This obviously appeared chaotic to outsiders. Also, if someone had a message in tongues but neither they nor anyone else present was able to interpret it, the message was not to be given (see

1 Cor. 14:22-30). Again, it was foolish to think that any benefit was given to the church if the message was unable to be understood.

2. The House of Cornelius

While Peter was still speaking these words, the Holy Spirit fell upon all those who heard the Word and those of the circumcision who believed were astonished...because the gift of the Holy Spirit had been poured out on the Gentiles also. For they heard them speak with tongues and magnify God... (Acts 10:44-46).

By this stage, the apostles were identifying the infilling of the Holy Spirit with speaking in tongues. These Jewish Christian believers were shocked that the people receiving the Baptism of the Holy Spirit were Gentiles. They had previously thought that people had to become a Jew to become a Christian. But now God was completely circumventing this and bringing in any who would receive Him.

3. The Ephesians

And when Paul had laid [his] hands on them, the Holy Spirit came upon them, and they spoke with tongues and prophesied (Acts 19:6).

The Ephesian believers, though only a small group at the beginning, rapidly grew to become one of the most significant churches of New Testament times. It began with the Baptism of the Holy Spirit as evidenced by speaking in tongues.

The final two examples of the Baptism of the Holy Spirit (from the Book of Acts) do not record the phrase "They spoke with tongues," but in light of the previous verses noted, and in light of other supporting Scripture, I think it's safe to conclude that they also spoke in tongues.

4. The Apostle Paul

Ananias went his way and entered the house; and laying his hands on him he said, "Brother Saul, the Lord Jesus, who appeared to you on the road as you came, has sent me that you may receive your sight and be filled with the Holy Spirit" (Acts 9:17).

As we read Paul's writings to the Corinthians regarding tongues, we see that his own personal testimony is, *"I speak in tongues more than you all"* (1 Cor. 14:18 NIV). Obviously somewhere down the line Paul received the gift of speaking in tongues. In light of the other New Testament examples, it is reasonable to assume that this occurred when Ananias laid hands on him in Acts 9:17.

Paul had witnessed some incredible supernatural occurrences prior to when Ananias laid hands on him: a light from Heaven, a voice from Heaven, a miracle of blindness, he fell to the ground, a vision of Ananias coming to him. Yet, none of these were evidence that he himself had actually received the Baptism of the Holy Spirit.

5. The Samaritans

Then they laid hands on them and they received the Holy Spirit (Acts 8:17).

Acts 8:5 begins the story of Philip the evangelist who had just been in the areas around Judea and Samaria, and his ministry had brought an enormous revival. Apostles Peter and John had been sent down to the Samaritan revival to inspect what was happening. Although it was a remarkable move of God, the statement is very clear in Acts 8:16 that, *"as yet He* [the Holy Spirit] *had fallen upon none of them."* This statement demands that the reception of the Holy Spirit be an event that is plainly and immediately observable. The same is true of other statements in the passage: *"They prayed for them that they might receive the Holy Spirit"* (Acts 8:15); and, *"Simon saw that through the laying on of the apostles' hands the Holy Spirit was given"* (Acts 8:18). All of these indicate a visible, definite descent of the Holy Spirit—sudden, emphatic, and obvious. The evidence was clearly *not* faith in Christ as Savior, nor baptism in water, nor great joy, nor answered prayer, nor miracles of healing, nor a sweeping revival. The Samaritans had all of these things in abundance, yet Luke boldly asserts that none of them had received the Holy Spirit in the baptism of power.

TONGUES: ENTRY TO THE SUPERNATURAL WORLD OF GOD

The entry point into the supernatural world of God has been reduced to the "least of the gifts": *tongues*. It is hotly contested because the power of the Holy Spirit is the key to a worldwide awakening to Christ. It is the power He promised us so that we are equipped to fulfill the Great Commission. To reduce the "evidence" any more is to dilute the experience and rob people of the opportunity of receiving the full power of God into their lives. This is why we must hold fast to this "ancient landmark" for which our forefathers braved so much opposition.

Conversely, speaking in other tongues is not necessarily a guarantee that a person is actually living a life baptized in the Spirit. Once a gift is given, God will not retract it. A person may fall from a life "on fire" for God, yet still be capable of speaking in tongues. It is a gift that comes with the initial infilling of the Spirit.

To remain Baptized in the Spirit should be the quest of every Christian. The early disciples were filled again and again with the Holy Spirit. It need not be a one-time experience. This powerful infilling can be the constant experience of every believer.

In *Experiencing the Presence of God*, Charles Finney tells of his initial experience of the power of God coming on him. He says that he immediately began witnessing to others. He found that just a few words would carry such conviction that many times people would repent and turn to Christ right then and there. However, he explained that if he found these results lacking, he would become distressed and so retreat to prayer to discover why. He would search his heart to understand why the Spirit had been grieved or quenched. Once he had cleared his heart of all offenses and felt again the power of Christ upon him, he would resume witnessing and preaching with the powerful results of many conversions.[6]

The highest purpose of the Baptism in the Spirit is so that we walk in the Spirit, being effective at bringing people to Christ.[7]

ENDNOTES

1. *Strong's Dictionary,* #G911.

2. Derek Prince, *Foundation Series, Volume 1: Sovereign World* (Derek Prince Ministries Publishing, 1966).

3. Pentecostals number second only to Roman Catholics in Christendom. There are one billion Catholics, 600 million Pentecostals, and 194 million Evangelicals. http://www.adherents.com/rel_USA.html#religions.

4. *Strong's Dictionary,* #G1411.

5. This is in spite of the facts that first century church believers spoke in tongues (see Acts 10:45-46), that apostle Paul admonished believers in First Corinthians 14:39 to *"not forbid speaking in tongues,"* and that there is absolutely no verse anywhere in the Bible that mentions, indicates, or even hints that this gift of the Holy Spirit and evidence of Baptism of the Holy Spirit was ever revoked from the Body.

6. Charles Finney, *Experiencing The Presence Of God* (Whitaker House, 2000).

7. How to live a life filled with the Holy Ghost is discussed in another teaching. This teaching is designed as an introduction to the initial infilling and baptism of the power of God.

FOUNDATION FOUR

Spiritual Gifts

LOVE IS THE GREAT MOTIVATOR of spiritual gifts. A minister feels compassion for the people he or she is called to serve. We love them. We want to heal them, to give them guidance, to lead them, to prophesy a great future for them. Love fans gifts into flame.

The gifts of the Holy Spirit are given to empower us to build the church. This means we increase it by adding more people to the Kingdom, and by causing growth in the believers. Sometimes I see things about people. Visions of these kinds seem to come easily to me in worship. Many times I tell people what I see. I occasionally prophesy over members in church. Sometimes they are new people. Some say they decided to stay because of that word spoken over them. This use of a gift plants people in God's house. One person reasoned that, "If this is where God is going to speak to me, I'm staying!" People want to be where God is moving, where He is speaking, healing, where He is active. Gifts build the church.

On the other hand, I used to find that I had no great sense of ease in healing the sick. It took a very real impartation of the Holy Spirit for that to happen through me. Yet this gifting has been getting stronger and stronger, so that we are now seeing many people healed in our services. The gifts of the Spirit can increase in our lives.

I don't attempt to heal the sick or offer any promise of healing when I pray for people unless I am conscious of the power of God to do that. Yet, remarkable healings from God take place when we lay hands on the sick. Cancers are healed, verified under medical examination. I have seen people delivered from many sicknesses and from comas—even infertile women healed so they could conceive, when the doctors had told them this would never happen because of medical conditions they had.

In fact, many miracles have happened over the years in this area. Yet prophecy rests on my life far more comfortably than healing. Whenever someone is to be healed through me, the Holy Spirit delivers that gift to me for use at that particular time. I know others who feel the same about healing as I do about prophecy. They love meeting someone who is sick. Their compassion for the sick is released through the gift in them.

THREE CATEGORIES OF GIFTS OF THE SPIRIT

The gifts of the Spirit (listed in First Corinthians 12) are divided into three categories:

1. Vocal gifts: Gifts of speech

2. Revelation gifts: Gifts of insight

3. Power gifts: Gifts of ability

Each category has three different forms. Thus, nine supernatural gifts are described in the First Corinthians passage.

Vocal gifts:

- Tongues

- Interpretation of tongues

- Prophecy

Revelatory gifts:

- Word of wisdom

- Word of knowledge

- Discerning of spirits

Power gifts:

- Faith

- Healings

- Miracles

SOME BACKGROUND

Before we examine each, let's look at what Jesus says about the Baptism of the Holy Spirit:

On the last day, that great day of the feast, Jesus stood and cried out, saying, "If anyone thirsts, let him come to Me and drink. He who believes in Me, as the Scripture has said, 'out of his heart will flow rivers of living water.'" But this He spoke concerning the Spirit, whom those believing in Him would receive... (John 7:37-39).

Perhaps you are thinking that you are born again, but a deep hunger for the Baptism of the Holy Spirit and spiritual gifts remains unsatisfied within. It is easy to receive the Baptism of the Holy Spirit. It is not difficult. It is simple and effortless. It is a beautiful gift of God (see Acts 2:38). It comes to us by grace, not by our efforts (see Gal. 3:2). We receive it using faith and trust, not by strain and struggling.

The first thing we must have, though, *is hunger and thirst for the Holy Spirit.* In John 7:37 Jesus says, *"If anyone thirsts, let him come to Me and drink."* We hunger for God and thirst for the Holy Spirit. We want more of God. We are hungry for Him, His Word and His Spirit. Our appetite for God must be strong. The degree of our thirsting is the degree we experience the Holy Spirit in our lives.

Second, we must expect nothing less than complete success. This is faith. Ask Jesus now to baptize you with the Holy Spirit. Faith takes from God what He has promised. Receive the Baptism now! Right now, pray, "Fill me with your Spirit now, Lord. I want more of You. Baptize me in the Holy Spirit today. This is Your will for me."

Third, speak in tongues. Acts 2:4 tells us that they *"began to speak."* Give voice to your new language. You ask...the Holy Spirit falls on you...you speak with new tongues. Speak, until out of your innermost being flow rivers of living water, just as Jesus promised.

The anointing is imparted in measure. God distributes a measure of the anointing on a group newly selected for leadership:

So the Lord said to Moses: "Gather to Me seventy men of the elders of Israel, whom you know to be the elders of the people and officers over them; bring them to the tabernacle of meeting, that they may stand there with you. Then I will come down and talk with you there. I will take of the Spirit that is upon you and will put the same upon them; and they shall bear the burden of the people with you, that you may not bear it yourself alone" (Numbers 11:16-17).

Once God did this, all of the elders receiving just a small portion of the anointing on Moses can't help but prophesy. They begin shouting the Word of God. Until this point, Moses is the only one with this anointing for leadership and government. God takes a portion of this great slab of anointing on him, then slices it into seventy pieces and drops one seventieth of a portion of the anointing on Moses onto each of the seventy elders. They don't know what's hit them. They fall down prophesying.

This also reveals the great capacity of Moses. He has been carrying around an anointing at least seventy times more powerful than on these elders. The anointing is so great upon him his face literally *shines*. He wears a veil so people can cope with being around him.

Joshua is concerned because two of the elders prophesying are not in the tabernacle. They're down by their tents. He wants to stop them. Moses, however, is completely unconcerned about trying to keep things religiously correct. He wants everyone to have the anointing and all to be prophesying.

The anointing has little respect for our religious traditions. God ignores our religious traditions. *For he whom God hath sent speaketh the words of God: for God giveth not the Spirit by measure unto him* (John 3:34 KJV).

THE MEASURE OF THE ANOINTING CAN GROW

The measure of the anointing on us grows as our capacity to carry it increases. David experiences three moments of the anointing increasing on his life.

The first occurs as a young lad of about sixteen in front of his parents and brothers in his hometown. The prophet Samuel pours a horn full of oil over the young man. His mind fills with visions of his future. This anointing takes him into the court of King Saul, who suffers from deep depression. David plays his music and the depression lifts. Saul's misery comes from demons. The music of David breaks the power of darkness, so Saul has him stay in the palace. Then David defeats Goliath. Saul promotes him to the position of general over the entire army.

However, as David grows in popularity, Saul grows in jealousy. He demotes young David to a captaincy over one thousand. The king's jealousy increases as he realizes David is God's choice to succeed him. He plots David's death several times, betraying him, chasing him around the desert. Time and again David has the opportunity to kill Saul, but he doesn't. He trusts his destiny into the hands of God; rather than work it out himself. He also has deep respect for the anointing. He knows God has anointed Saul. David is unwilling to cause him harm. Saul's troubles only increase. He refuses to get his life right with God. In this backslidden state, he consults witches for guidance.

Finally, sadly, King Saul and his son Jonathan are killed in battle. Immediately after this, David receives the second measure of anointing. David has assembled his own private army and has repeatedly brought destruction to the Philistines (the enemies of Israel). The tribe of Judah decide they want David as their king. He is anointed king over Judah.

They anoint him at Hebron from where he rules for the next seven and a half years until the remainder of Israel recognize him as the man that God had chosen to rule the whole nation. This is the third and greatest measure of the anointing that falls upon David. David finally enters his destiny as the ruler of Israel.

Our journey into greater measures of the anointing involves greater development of our character. This increases our ability to carry the touch of God. This is not an easy thing. Many who have carried a great anointing have not finished well. The anointing brings with it many pressures. Our emotional, moral, mental, relational, and physical capacities must be strong.

THE ANOINTING REVIVES US

The anointing revives our spirit. In biblical times, when guests arrive at the home of their host after a long day in Middle Eastern sun, they are greeted with a basin of water to wash their hands and feet. Then they are anointed with fresh aromatic oil, which revitalizes them. This is exactly the same impact of the moving of the Holy Spirit:

> *Repent therefore and be converted, that your sins may be blotted out, so that times of refreshing may come from the presence of the Lord* (Acts 3:19).

As we discussed in Foundation One, *Repentance*, the meaning of the word *refreshing*, (Greek, *anapsuxis*), literally means "a recovery of breath, revival, cooling, refreshing, recovery from the effects of heat."

In Second Kings 4, we find the story of a "great woman" who makes room for God and therefore eventually receives a "reviving" miracle. The prophet Elisha passes by her house regularly. She gives him food, but the man has to keep moving because there is no room in her house for him to stay.

This is much like God with the Church. He visits but can't stay. There's simply no room. There's no room conceptually, emotionally, or just in the schedule of the church; there's no time when God can move. Some church services are so full and the times so rigid that even if God does want to move, everyone leaves because there is just not enough time for God.

Well, the woman in Second Kings decides to "make room" for God. After she has made the extra room in the house, the prophet comes and stays. He wants to reward her. He promises her she will have a child within twelve months. The woman has been barren to this point. She finds his promise difficult to accept. Yet within twelve months she gives birth to a young boy. The child grows. As a teenager he goes to the fields, helping his father with the harvest. In the middle of the day the heat of the sun takes its toll on the lad. He faints. He is carried to the lap of his mother. He dies. The mother lays the boy in that same room she has made for the prophet. She rushes to the man of God and asks him to come. The prophet comes. He lies on the child, breathing into him. Breath returns to the young body. The boy revives!

Many Christians have been burned out working in the harvest. Many faint in the heat of the work of God. Revival comes when we *make room for God*. We need fresh encounters with God. The anointing comes on us again. We revive.

RELEASING THE ANOINTING

The power of God does *not* depend on our power. It depends on our *powerlessness*. Paul gloried in his weaknesses rather than in his strengths, so that the power of God continues to *rest on him* (see 2 Cor. 12:9). When we think we can do it, or have to do it, then we rely on ourselves. If we feel we can't do it, then we rely on God. When we use great personal effort to accomplish a task and rely on ourselves to do the job, we are using our power, not God's. When we walk in faith we walk in rest. ...*whoever believes will not act hastily* (Isa. 28:16).

In rest, we cease from our works. We trust in the power of God (see Heb. 4:10). We rest in the Lord. We act on His prompting. The anointing is released through us as we follow the inclinations of the Holy Spirit. He inclines us to do things through our emotions, through our thoughts, our desires, and motivations. Without the power of God, we are on our own. Trying to build a spiritual Kingdom through the "arm of flesh" will kill us. It is imperative we don't become blockages to the Spirit and the anointing. It is imperative we release the power of God to build the Kingdom of God.

WHY THE ANOINTING IS BLOCKED

The anointing power of God upon our lives can be blocked by unbelief and by fear.

UNBELIEF

Many of us simply don't believe that the inclination we have is actually from God. We say, "It's just me." Well, who else is it going to be?! We expect the roof to split wide open, an angel descends in a fiery pillar, points his finger at us, takes our tongue and waggles it up and down, making us do something we have nothing to do with ourselves. No, God moves *through* us, through who *we are*, and what *we* feel. He doesn't move separately from us. The inclinations of the Holy Ghost and the pictures He places in our imagination can seem so very natural and obvious that we find it difficult to believe it's actually God. The leadings of the Holy Spirit are unassuming, humble, *"still and small"* (see 1 Kings 19:12).

FEAR

When we are fearful in our spirit, we can't receive or release the power of the Holy Spirit. Bound by the fear of others, we will never move in the Holy Spirit. Attempting to fulfill the expectations we think others have of us, we will ignore the Holy Spirit, and try to please people. If we are intent on maintaining the popularity of the people and keeping a respectable reputation, we will not do those things the Spirit prompts, because they *"are foolishness to those who are perishing* [the natural man]" (see 1 Cor. 1:18).

So, for example, if we are unable to speak in tongues because we are embarrassed, we have a fear problem. We will not be able to move with the Holy Spirit. When the Holy Spirit moves on us, we do things we would not do naturally. If we will just stop caring so much what people think, we will follow the Spirit. Our "natural man" is proud and does not easily submit to the Spirit. It is humbling in every way to obey the Spirit. When we respond to the Spirit, we learn to take action in the Spirit. This sometimes means doing what seems unusual to us. Following those inclinations, though, releases the Spirit.

EXTRAORDINARY MANIFESTATIONS

This truth needs to be said again so that you really understand: in this great move of God reviving Christians all around the world, many extraordinary things take place. These things are not new. Throughout the Bible and throughout church history, these same manifestations were occurring.

In Genesis 26:18, we read that Isaac dug again the wells his father Abraham had dug. Our "fathers" in the faith have dug wells of the Holy Spirit that released joy, revival, healing, and powerful demonstrations of God's ability to meet the needs of this world.

> *The church today needs to be aroused, to be awakened, to be filled with a spirit of glory, for she is failing in the modern world.* —Martin Lloyd Jones[1]

John Wesley records some of the outpourings of the Spirit in the 1700s. In *The Journal of the Rev. John Wesley*, Wesley recounts:

At New Year's 1739, George Whitfield, my brother Charles, three others, and I, with about sixty of our brethren, were present at a love feast in Fetter Lane. About three in the morning as we were continuing in prayer, the power of God came upon us so mightly that many cried out in holy joy, while others were knocked to the ground. As soon as we were recovered little from awe and amazement at the presence of God, we broke out in one voice, (of praise).

Thursday at Newgate…one, then another, and another sunk to the Earth. They dropped on every side as if thunderstruck. One of them cried aloud. We besought God on her behalf, and He turned her heaviness into joy.

Friday evening, I went to a society at Wapping weary in body and faint in spirit….After I had finished preaching and was earnestly inviting all sinners to enter into the holiest by this new and living way, many of those who heard began to call upon God with strong cries and tears. Some sank down having no strength remaining in them. Others tremble and quaked exceedingly. Some were torn with a kind of convulsive motion in every part of their bodies often so violently that sometimes 4 or 5 persons could not hold one of them. I have seen epileptic fits and hysteria, but none of them were like these. I immediately prayed that God would not allow those who were weak to be offended.[2]

Daniel Rowland served as one of the preachers in the Welsh revival. In *The Manners of the Antient Christians* in a letter to his friend George Whitfield, Rowland relates:

While one is praying another is laughing, some howl and beat their hands together, others are weeping and groaning; and others are groveling on the ground in a swoon, making various kinds of antic postures, then they all laugh at once, and continue laughing for about half an hour. Such crying out and heart breaking groans, silent weeping and holy joy and shouts of rejoicing, I never saw (before). 'Tis very common when he preaches for scores to fall down by the power of the Word, pierced and wounded by the love of God, and sights and beauty of the excellency of Jesus… Some lie on the floor for hours, some praising and admiring Jesus; others wanting for words to utter. You might read the language of a heart running over with love in their heavenly looks, their eyes sparkling with the fire of love and joy and solid rest in God.[3]

Another writes of those times of revival in the 1700s,

Some souls in this meeting were feasting at their heavenly Fathers table. Some were drunk, and that with the best wine, namely the Holy Spirit, God's peace, God's love shed abroad in their hearts by the Holy Ghost. Some prominent people scorn and deride this, but it is the substance of religion.[4]

The writers continue in their defense that it was a work of God:

It is not only by means of outward manifestations, such as shouting , jumping, laughing, that I conclude that God is in the Church visiting His people. Apart from the heavenly inclination on their spirits inciting that their tongues to a lively praising of God, this fire burns in the life and behaviour of so many of them…They are zealous not for secondary matters of faith, but for the essential values of salvation. Faith and love are the chief graces they cry for.[5]

During the second Great Awakening of 1798-1832, the reviving influences of the Holy Spirit brought great moves of the Spirit. Peter Cartwright, a frontiersman in Kentucky, in his autobiography, *Backwoods Preacher*, speaks of the "mighty power of God" manifesting in his meetings:

In the midst of our controversies on the subject of the powerful exercises among the people under preaching, a new exercise has broken out among us, called the jerks, which was overwhelming in its effects upon the bodies and minds of the people. No matter whether they were saints or sinners, they wood be taken under a warm song or sermon, and seized with a convulsive jerking all over, which they could not by any possibility avoid, and the more they resisted the more they jerked. I have seen more than 500 persons (in this state) at one time in my large congregations....To see those proud young gentlemen, and young ladies, dressed in their silks, jewellery, and prunella, from top to toe, take the jerks, would often cause me to laugh. The first jerk or so would see their fine bonnets, caps, and combs fly; and so sudden would be the jerking of the head that their long loose hair would crack almost as loud as a wagoner's whip.[6]

In his *Sermons of Rev. C.H. Spurgeon of London*, C.H. Spurgeon speaks of his experiences of when the Spirit comes:

Observe how sovereign the operations of God are...He may in one district work a revival, and persons may be stricken down, and made to cry aloud, but in another place there may be crowds, and yet all may be still and quiet, as though no deep excitement existed at all...He can bless as he wills and he will bless as He wills. Let us not dictate to God. Many a blessing has been lost by Christians not believing it to be a blessing, because it did not come in the particular shape they had conceived to be proper and right.[7]

In *Annals and Statistics of the United Presbyterian Church*, William Blair comments on the manifestations, and in particular the striking down of people, or prostrations, or what we would call resting in the Spirit, or falling out. He says:

Too little as well as too much has been made of the singular physical features of this great revival. By some they are regarded as abnormal and excessive. I do not think so. They have accompanied all revivals...I care not what the sceptics may say, or little faith Christians, who have no confidence in the extraordinary influences of the Holy Spirit. I believe as firmly as I believe in my own existence, that the Holy Ghost would never have permitted His work to be entangled with such perplexing and seemingly incredible phenomena, had He not had a most important end to serve by them.[8]

These wells of joy and manifestations of the power of God touching people's emotions and setting them free have already been dug by our forefathers in the faith. However, these same wells have become blocked, clogged, and ineffective, just like the wells of Abraham. In his day the Philistines had plugged up the wells, well aware that without water it is impossible to maintain any kind of livelihood in the desert. Without water, Abraham's family would be unable to stay in the area if they wanted to survive. The record says that Isaac dug again the wells his father Abraham had dug (see Gen. 26:18).

The Philistines employed three different means to block up the wells of their enemies. They poured dirt down the well, or stones, or simply threw in a dead animal that poisoned the water.

Too much of the world in the church kills off the river of God. When the church seeks her thrills in the world rather than in the Lord, she dies.

Rocks and stones are the hard, unforgiving, judgmental attitudes the church drifts into, posturing from a self-righteous platform, pointing accusing fingers everywhere. This defeats mercy. It only blocks, once again, the wells of salvation.

Dead animals are people in our relationships who are negative, backslidden, critical. They hold a negative influence over our lives. The life of Heaven is blocked by these influences in our lives.

LAUGHTER AND JOY

The name *Isaac* means "laughter." Laughter is one of the great results of the move of the Spirit. People discover joy they never realized was available. Churches have sanctified weeping, but frown on laughter. We've disallowed joy. Laughter literally unplugs blocked wells. Suddenly the river of Heaven is pouring out. People are set free from hardness, from worldliness and stuff that binds them. I've watched thousands on the floor laughing, then crying, laughing then crying, etc. This healing and freeing process is literally "digging again the wells" our fathers dug. And laughter (Isaac) can do it! Laughter is not the only "new" or unusual expression people discover under the power of the Holy Spirit.

A few years ago it was irreverent to clap hands in church. When that became accepted, people felt like dancing. Some fell on their face in worship before God. Some leaders banned this from their churches. Apparently this was inappropriate for the house of God. Then people began raising their hands and speaking and singing in tongues all at the same time. This again was condemned by many, rejected on all kinds of scriptural grounds. But really, this happens every time something "new" comes into the church. We have been hopelessly guilty throughout the age of rejecting anything that smacks of "new."

RESISTING THE NEW

The church sanctifies the past and condemns the future, holding out a beachhead of resistance to the new, raising alarms of all kinds in the name of holiness. However, generally it is simply fear of losing respectability. These days, it is quite acceptable to clap, dance, lift hands, and sing in tongues in many churches. The Internet is full of such images, which are used by advertising companies to sell products. We have become respectable. We don't realize how stuck in that respect-ability we are until the Lord invades our world with something "new." Something we haven't seen before. It looks foolish!

But the things of the Spirit *are foolishness* to the natural man (see 1 Cor. 2:14). After we do something in the Spirit a few times, our flesh imitates. It's no longer a spiritual reality at all. It becomes empty religious activity. We grow cold in heart. We need reviving. God is reviving us. He brings unusual things to us so we learn to step out and do whatever the Spirit tells us without fear. When the Almighty God of Heaven and earth touches our lives, we respond in ways not normal.

On the Day of Pentecost the apostles are mocked by the crowd. They appear drunk. It's only nine o'clock in the morning. They seem incoherent, joyful, and delirious all at the same time. Yet, this was the birthing of the Church! One of the men begins to speak. Three thousand devout religious people turn to Christ through the anointed preaching of Peter the apostle.

RELEASE THE SPIRIT WITHIN!

If we are unprepared to receive the Spirit in whatever way the Father chooses to send Him, then we will have no chance of releasing the Spirit to those God has called us to. It is vital that we are *ministers of the Spirit*. Anything else does not get the job done. It is chaff, and the wind of God blows it away. We have come up with all kinds of substitutes by which we are meant to reach the world without the Spirit. Yet none of these actually produce the results God looks for. People are not born again by human endeavor, but by the Spirit: *That which is born of the flesh is flesh, and that which is born of the Spirit is spirit* (John 3:6).

THE VOCAL GIFTS

There are three vocal gifts: tongues, interpretation of tongues, and prophecy.

1. NEW LANGUAGES (TONGUES)

Tongues is the evidence that we have received the Baptism of the Holy Spirit. Ephesians 1:13 says the Holy Spirit is given as the seal of our salvation. The baptism confirms we are saved. We are not saved *by* the Baptism of the Holy Spirit and speaking in tongues. However, the Baptism of the Holy Spirit and the subsequent speaking in tongues is *confirmation* of our salvation. It assures us that, at the Second Coming, we will be raised up (raptured) with Christ in the resurrection of believers.

In Foundation Three we discussed in detail the five examples of believers receiving the Baptism of the Holy Spirit that are found in the Book of Acts. In three of these, it is recorded that they spoke in tongues. Paul's Baptism in the Holy Spirit is one of the other two occasions where there is no mention of whether people instantly spoke in tongues or not. However, we know that Paul did speak in tongues. He says later in First Corinthians 14:18, *"I thank God, I speak in tongues more than you all!"*

The fifth example is the Samaritan believers. They experienced a powerful manifestation of the power of God when they were baptized in the Holy Spirit. Simon the sorcerer, obviously familiar to supernatural phenomena, was so astounded that he offered money to receive ability to do the same (see Acts 8:14-24). The fact that it could be immediately seen and heard, taken with the consistent experience of the people in the other four cases, means that this manifestation is easily the gift of tongues in action.

As mentioned previously, there are three kinds of tongues (supernatural languages): other languages, unknown languages, and angelic languages.

Other Languages

These are languages that disciples in the Upper Room spoke on the Day of Pentecost. They spoke in "other languages" they had previously never learned, not just one language, but many, varied languages. *They communicated supernaturally the message God wanted people to hear.* This supernatural sign, combined with Peter's preaching, brought instant conversion to three thousand devout Jews. This was going to be one of the most difficult groups to ever convert. However, through the power of the Holy Spirit, it happened.

I hope you sense the desperate need for us to lay hold of even this simplest of gifts. It has been called "the least" of gifts by some Christians, though this description appears nowhere in Scripture. Yet consider its impact on the Day of Pentecost, when three thousand devout religious men were saved. If "the least" of gifts can accomplish this, *what remarkable things can the greatest of gifts do?* I believe we are experiencing only pale semblances of what the Holy Spirit can really do. But, *powerful days are ahead as we pursue these gifts of the Spirit!* Paul urges us in First Corinthians 14:1 to *"...desire spiritual gifts."*

Churches have been badgered by in-house contentions over the gifts of the Spirit. While we squabble, souls perish. In the environment of unbelief, disunity, and resistance, the Spirit has been unable to manifest these amazing gifts of power, signs, and wonders through us, His people.

This first gift of tongues, "other languages," does not require interpretation. It speaks directly to the ears of a person in their own tongue. The speaker expresses the message supernaturally in a language never learned.

Unknown Languages

For he who speaks in a tongue does not speak to men but to God, for no one understands him; however, in the spirit he speaks mysteries (1 Corinthians 14:2).

This Scripture passage in First Corinthians states this gift is intended not for others, but for God. No interpretation is necessary. God understands what the believer is praying, even though no one else does. Praying in the Spirit edifies the believer himself (see 1 Cor. 14:4). We are built up in our most holy faith, Jude 20 says, *"by praying in the Holy Spirit."* We need to use this gift freely in worship, singing and prayer, during church services, prayer meetings, and in private worship and intercession.

Speaking in unknown tongues is vital to effective prayer and worship. Paul encourages us to speak and to sing with the spirit, and with understanding (see 1 Cor. 14:15).

Angelic Languages

Angelic tongues are communications *from* God *to* people. These are unintelligible (to earthly ears) messages. Even though these "tongues" seem unintelligible, they actually are a definite language. It is the supernatural language of angels (see 1 Cor. 13:1). These are messages from God, via angels, spoken by a believer to the church when it is gathered together.

Angelic messages are authoritative, bold proclamations from God. Angelic tongues need interpretation so we can comprehend what God is saying. The Bible instructs the person giving the message to pray they also interpret (see 1 Cor. 14:13). If they are unable to do this, the Bible says they're not to give the message unless someone present can interpret. Otherwise, the message has no meaning and therefore no power to edify the church. These unearthly, heavenly languages, need spiritual "decoding."

In forty years of ministry, I have been in a lot of "Spirit-filled" meetings and have seen a lot of wild things. We need to move in the Holy Spirit in a way that is perceived by anyone looking on as sane. The Holy Spirit wants to build the Church and bring lost people to Christ. All the manifestations of the Holy Spirit should achieve this.

First Corinthians 14:32 says, *"The spirits of prophets are subject to the prophets."* This means inspiration is controllable. If not, it is suspect. Even when people are seemingly overwhelmed by the Holy Spirit, they are still able to take control of what is happening at any time. One of the fruits of the Holy Spirit is self-control (see Gal. 5:23). The Holy Spirit gives self-control. He doesn't remove self-control.

This gift is also a sign and a wonder to people who don't believe (see 1 Cor. 14:22). One of my best friends came to Christ after hearing people speak in tongues, worshiping God. He thought it was the most beautiful thing he had ever heard!

2. INTERPRETATION OF TONGUES

This is closely connected with speaking in angelic tongues. This gift interprets angel's messages to the church.

> *For he who speaks in a tongue does not speak to men but to God, for no one understands him; however, in the spirit he speaks mysteries* (1 Corinthians. 14:2).

These "mysteries" need to be communicated to congregations in terms that are easily understood. The person delivering messages in tongues to the church should wait for the right moment in the worship service. We are also told to pray that we ourselves might deliver the interpretation. If we are unable to interpret, we must be first aware there is someone present who can. As I said previously, if no interpreter is present, the message in tongues shouldn't be given.

Paul calls tongues "mysteries." To interpret a message in tongues is to interpret mysteries. Supernatural interpretation is vital. So much of life can be filed under "mysteries." We have a supernatural ability in this gift to interpret what is mysterious to people. Gifts of the Spirit have much wider potential than just corporate worship gatherings. Interpretation of tongues is the ability to interpret mysteries in life. In delivering the revelation of the New Testament, Paul refers to the "mysteries of the ages," which have been hidden since the beginning. This man, who *"spoke in tongues more than you all,"* brings the interpretation of mysteries that relate to us those magnificent purposes of God through history and time.

This gift of the interpretation of tongues can also be used in our prayer times. Romans 8:26 tells us that the Holy Spirit prays through us. Sometimes these prayers are completely in the gift of tongues. We can ask for understanding of what we are praying. The Spirit often speaks to us in our personal lives through tongues. We can interpret in prayer and become aware of what the Spirit is saying to us. If we need wisdom from God about anything in our lives, we should spend time speaking in tongues. God brings wisdom to us through the gift of interpretation.

The interpretation of mysteries has been something God has gifted his servants with down through the ages and achieved incredible results through this. In Genesis, Joseph interprets the dreams of people in his world. When he reveals the meaning of dreams the King has had, he is promoted from the prison to the throne in the palace in a day, and he ensures that Egypt becomes amongst the most powerful nations on Earth. Just because of one moment of interpretation of a mystery! Again we see how important it is to never underestimate the far-reaching impact of the gifts of the Holy Spirit.

3. PROPHECY

Paul elevates this gift above all others, because it builds up the church:

> *He who speaks in a tongue edifies himself, but he who prophesies edifies the church. I wish you all spoke with tongues, but even more that you prophesied; for he who prophesies is greater than he who speaks with tongues, unless indeed he interprets, that the church may receive edification* (1 Corinthians 14:4-5).

Paul's passion and divine purpose was to build the church. He says this gift is to be earnestly desired (coveted) because of its powerful ability to strengthen saints.

However, a person with the gift of prophecy is not necessarily a prophet. Prophets foretell future events with accurate detail. Times, names, dates, places, past, and future events are clearly revealed to the person in this ministry. A person with the gift of prophecy does not "major on details" such as above, but speaks in general terms. *The specifics are in the ears of the hearers.* The hearers understand clearly what the Lord is saying to them regarding the details of their lives, even though no specifics are mentioned in the prophecy.

Prophecy **confirms** to people things they already feel. It crystallizes and clarifies their thoughts. It jolts the realization that their impressions are actually from God. We should be a little suspicious of a prophecy attempting to be motivational, getting people doing something they've never thought. Prophecy confirms God's voice to people. It doesn't replace His voice.

True prophecy is always motivated by love. Love for people. All the gifts of the Spirit are given to profit everyone in every way. *But the manifestation of the Spirit is given to each one for the profit of all* (1 Cor. 12:7).

The gifts are not only motivated *by* love but also given *in* love. If the spirit of a prophecy is anything but this, it is not right. It builds up. It doesn't tear down.

I've known of critical people expressing their opinions through their supposed gift of prophecy. The very people doing this begin to imagine this is how everyone operates gifts of the Spirit. It opens the door for self-deception. In addition, the church is not built up and boosted, but rather put down, grieving the Spirit. True prophecy brings God to a gathering. It does not subtract from the atmosphere, but adds to it. If prophecy condemns people, it is not from the Lord. The anointing descends when prophecy comes. People rise in victory, praise, and worship. They are lifted into awe before God. A heightened sense of God covers a congregation after a genuine word from God is delivered.

In Part

The gift of prophecy is only "in part" (see 1 Cor. 13:9). It is not perfect or complete. This means prophecy is susceptible to mixture. When we're young Christians and first use this gift, we often know when to start but not when to stop! We include thoughts of our own. Our latest revelation creeps in. We need to grow in expressing ourselves well through spiritual gifts. The mixture should be becoming less of us and more of Him. We seek to excel. Staying within the anointing becomes a constant pursuit. Sensitivity to the Holy Spirit and simple obedience to Him are essential for us to be skillful ministers of the Spirit. We need to say no more and no less than what He has given. We say what He gives and no more.

Prophecy is for *edification, exhortation, and comfort, to build up, challenge, and encourage.* Here's an example of what a prophecy should sound like:

> You are my children, I know, you each by name, I have called you, saved you, and brought you into My family [i.e. edification, building up]. Therefore, take My love to the world. Seek out those who are lonely and confused and freely give them what I have given you [i.e. exhortation, challenge]. And I will be with you, supply all your needs, and confirm your words, for I am for you. Therefore who can be against you [i.e. comfort, giving hope, and promise].

REVELATION GIFTS

There are another three gifts of the Spirit, all relating to revelation. *Gifts of revelation reveal things hidden to the natural mind.* They uncover secrets that need discovery. They reveal to us ways of accomplishing things beyond normal means. These gifts equip ministers and believers with insight so we are not working in the dark.

Let's examine each.

1. WORD OF KNOWLEDGE

A "word of knowledge" is when we receive information that we could not have gotten any other way other than from the Holy Spirit.

Elisha is the prophet in Israel. Through the gift of the word of knowledge, God shows him the plans of the king of Syria to ambush Israel. Elisha uncovers these secret plans, including the time and place, and shares them with the king of Israel. The Syrians are thwarted again and again. The Syrian king thinks it must be a spy among his own men telling the king of Israel their plans. He demands that the traitor reveal himself. However, his men tell him it is none of his aides, but rather it is the prophet in Israel, Elisha (see 2 Kings 6:8-12). The Syrian king tries to kill Elisha, but fails, and so the nation is saved by a simple gift of the word of knowledge.

In John 4 we read the story of Jesus traveling in Galilee. He passes through Samaria, a place where Jewish people are despised. The pure-bred Jews considered the Samaritans a mongrel race, impure stock defiling themselves by intermarrying with heathen nations. Orthodox Hebrews had expelled them from settlements in Judea.

Jesus is tired. He stops at a well. It happens to be Jacob's well. A woman has come to draw water. As far as the common culture of the day is concerned this counts as two strokes against her. Not only is she a woman, but a Samaritan too. The daily prayers of a rabbi included thanks to God that he was not born a woman. Besides this, the woman has earned a soiled reputation in town. We assume this, because there is a well in the town itself, while Jacob's well is some distance down the road out of town. The other village women have ostracized her. Wells are common meeting places for the women. They gather, talk, laugh, and gossip. Apparently this particular woman is not welcome.

Jesus sits by the well. He begins talking to her. He has a word of knowledge—He knows something about her that no one else but God knows. He tells her she has had five husbands and the one she is living with now is not her husband. She is stunned that this stranger knows this about her. Jesus does not condemn her. She immediately assumes He is the Messiah. Even though Jesus shows that He knows this about her, He is non-condemning. This mercy sets her free. She believes, and accepts Christ as the Messiah. She is set free through forgiveness.

She rushes into the city telling everyone about Jesus. Many Samaritans come out to see Him. When they hear Him, the entire city comes out and believes in Jesus. This astonishing revival all begins with a simple word of knowledge. Neither does it finish here. In Acts, Philip brings an enormous revival to these Samaritans who had believed in Christ several years before. Now the evangelist Philip takes them further, bringing the Baptism of the Holy Spirit and miracles to these people.

Through one small word of knowledge, Jesus ushered in an amazing revival to Samaria. The power of moving in the Holy Spirit is not to be underestimated! We must become greater ministers of the Spirit.

2. WORD OF WISDOM

No amount of education, no number of degrees can be substituted for the gift of a "word of wisdom." It enables us to know *how* to apply answers to any situation. The word of wisdom brings healing to broken relationships, saves thousands of dollars and endless court battles, because this gift brings wisdom; it supplies us with the way to solve difficult situations. God has ways of answering problems that may never enter our mind. If we are alive in the Holy Spirit, a word of wisdom supplies answers to difficulties impossible for the natural person to understand.

King Solomon is considered among the wisest people of history. He is also easily among the wealthiest. People traveled far, not only to see the splendor of Israel's king, but also to hear his wisdom. The queen of Sheba was struck breathless with the wonder of it all. Solomon's wisdom was famous throughout the world. The same God who gave Solomon this wisdom *is the God we are connected with today.* That same gift of wisdom is available today. Solomon's was a gift from God. He pursued it and found it. Like him, we too need to seek wisdom as a number one priority.

> *Get wisdom! Get understanding! Do not forget, nor turn away from the words of my mouth. Do not forsake her, and she will preserve you; Love her, and she will keep you. Wisdom is the principal thing; Therefore get wisdom. And in all your getting, get understanding* (Proverbs 4:5-7).

A famous story from First Kings 3:16-28 shows the wisdom of Solomon in action. Two women, both prostitutes, approach him with a unique problem. During the night, one had rolled over in her sleep, smothering her baby. The child died. She secretly exchanged her dead child for the living child of the other woman, apparently sleeping in the same room. As morning dawned, the woman recognized her living child being nursed by her colleague. She also recognizes the dead child lying next to her and knows it is not hers. She accuses the woman of stealing her baby. The woman denies it.

They bring their case to the king. Solomon hears the arguing women, then brings his judgment to solve their dilemma. He commands the child to be cut in two so they receive half each! The mother of the dead child agrees. The mother of the living child, even though she may lose him, cannot bear to see her baby killed. She cries out in anguish, "Spare the child, spare the child. She can have him!" Better the child live in the arms of a stranger than perish under the sword, she thinks. Her attitude shows she is obviously the true mother. Solomon returns the babe to his mother's arms. The other woman is punished. This is the word of wisdom in action: fast, simple answers to extremely complex problems.

3. DISCERNING OF SPIRITS

The New Testament minister should be able to discern what God is doing. We are to understand the moving of the Holy Spirit and what He is doing. We should know what the "mood" of the Spirit is. We should be able to discern the atmosphere of a place, whether good or bad. Demons try to restrict the moving of the Spirit; they try to hinder the release of faith, prayer, fellowship, and worship. We should be aware of any demon activity and deal with it in the name of Jesus, so that we pray with intelligence and impact.

The gift of discerning of spirits is given so we also discern the motivation behind people's actions. When we gain this kind of understanding, we're able to deal with life with our eyes open. This is exactly what these gifts of revelation are for: *the revealing of those things hidden to the natural person.*

With Love

It is important to remember that all these gifts of the Spirit are to be ministered with love. If I understand people's spirits, I can help them, even though they may be unwilling to uncover it themselves. A gift like this is not just for prying into people's worlds for the sake of accusing them of wrongdoing. It is to gain insight so we are able to bring solutions to problems.

All these gifts work in the environment of faith. John 7:38-39 says that those who *believe* will *receive* and *release* the Spirit. Faith is always linked with a willingness to step out in God. When we are unwilling to do something, we will never see how it could be possible. As soon as we are willing, even if we don't know how we are going to accomplish it, we will find a way. However, as long as we are unwilling to step out, not believing we can do it, we will find reasons why it can't be done.

If we are willing to do something, and we step out to do something for God, the power of the Spirit will flow through us. When we resist a positive idea, and refuse to get involved in doing anything, we become spectators. We watch from the sidelines, becoming critical, never attaining any goals of our own. The people who say *yes* and show a willing heart to help, to work, and to act, always find faith and those reasons why "it *can* be done."

Presence of Angels

The gift of discerning of spirits also reveals the presence of angels and their purpose. In the early 1980s, our church experienced rapid growth. Literally hundreds of people were joining our church. We had also planted several other churches in the city. Each week on a Friday afternoon, the pastors of those churches and our own pastors came together to pray. One particular Friday, angels were also present. I had never seen angels before or even sensed them like I did that day. I knew they were doing something, but I couldn't understand what it was. That night was our weekly prayer meeting. Here again, I became aware of angels. They were moving quickly around the room. They had rods in their hands. Yet I couldn't understand what they were doing.

Then, on Sunday in our morning worship service, once more I became aware of the same angels moving among the congregation. Finally I got it. The rods in their hands were for measuring. I had read of angels measuring temples and rivers in Ezekiel and the Book of Revelation. Here they were measuring our church! On Friday they had measured our leadership. On Friday night they had measured our prayer meeting. Now, on Sunday morning, they were measuring our worship. The people were measured on the way in and on the way out of church. Our attitudes, effectiveness, desire, faith, vision, and obedience were all under the scrutiny of God. I related this to the church. We were excited. We knew God was visiting us. We were getting ready for something.

Let me explain that during these times I did not actually *see* angels with my physical eyes. I simply "saw" that angels were present. It was like seeing within seeing. A few months later I was attending a conference in another city. Meanwhile, our church had continued to grow. We were holding four services every Sunday and looking at new buildings to accommodate this growth. However, we had encountered major resistance from the local council. At the end of one of the conference meetings, the speaker asked people to stand if the message had touched them and they wanted to receive from God.

Chris and I were at the back of the hall, not having being particularly involved with the meeting. But both Chris and I did want to hear from God, so we stood. As soon as we did, I had an experience I had never had before and have never had since. I was face to face with an angel. This time I was literally seeing an angel. His face was the most beautiful I had ever seen. He was like a flame with a body. He was about the same height as I was. His head turned toward Heaven. At the same time he drew a sword from his side. He lifted it high, looked back in my face and let the sword fall on my shoulder like he was commissioning me. He then pronounced just one word: "Ready!" It was all over within seconds. I was breathless.

I knew this related to the time angels with the measuring rods had visited our church. I also knew it related to our current building changeover plans. Within two weeks we received permission to proceed into our building.

My conclusion was that the angels had measured us to see if we were ready for greater growth. Then a tailor-made situation had been created for that. The new building was that situation. Although we saw the council being the cause of delays, perhaps God had been waiting for us to be in a place where we could cope with greater growth. We operated far more effectively once in that new building. Our church planting exploded all over Australia and began to reach major cities around the world.

We need to understand when, why, and what God is doing. This is how we keep in step with Him. The gift of discerning of spirits is how we achieve this.

POWER GIFTS

There are three power gifts: faith, healings, and miracles.

1. FAITH

All the gifts of the Spirit are qualities that should be active in our lives as Spirit-filled Christians. Some gifts will be more alive in us than others. They seem easy for us to move in. For me, the gift of faith is a major motivation. It weaves its way through every area of my life.

Ever since I became a Christian, I have felt a strong attraction to faith. In my early days as a young believer, I read everything I could lay my hands on about it. I listened to all the preaching I could that filled me with faith in God.

The gift of faith is the ability to believe in positive results under impossible circumstances. Faith believes God will bring to pass things that people don't believe will happen. The gift of faith *makes things happen* that would not otherwise have occurred. The gift of faith knows it *has* something *before* it even exists. Faith imparts the assurance that *nothing is impossible.* This gift lived in Joshua and Caleb about Canaan. It lived in David running toward Goliath. It lived in Peter walking on water. It lived in him again speaking to a cripple at the Gate Beautiful telling him, "Rise and walk."

The Principles of Faith

There are certain principles of faith. These principles need to be active for this gift to work.

The Word of God is the food for this gift. Faith lives when it hears the word of God. *Faith speaks.* This is how faith creates. Through words. Paul speaks of the *"word of faith which we preach"* (Rom. 10:8). Second Corinthians 4:13 relates the Psalmist saying *"I believed and therefore I spoke."* Faith's first expression is speech. It prophesies something will come to pass. It commands things to happen. It speaks to circumstances, inanimate objects and situations, commanding changes. And changes happen. Faith gets the job done. Hebrews 11 attests abundantly to that. Faith hears the *rhema* of God, then acts. God shows complete contempt for those who hear the word of God, but do not believe it or act upon it.

When we hear the word of God, we must believe it, receive it, see it, speak it, and act it. This is the normal requirement on any believer. If we are unable to do these things, we hinder the gift of faith. The gift of faith is identified by an unnatural, supernatural boldness in prayer and preaching. Faith deals boldly with people and their problems.

- Faith is visionary: it views the future with absolute assurance and hope.

- Faith thinks positively: it hates negativity.

- Faith feeds on who we are in Christ and what our potential in Him is.

- Faith speaks to other people, to situations, and often to itself.

- Faith dreams and meditates on the finished results of prayer. It does not dwell on anxieties.

- Faith lifts others, injecting faith into their lives.

- Faith imparts the ability to believe and trust God.

- Faith proclaims God's goodness. It sees God as good.

- Faith is smiling, happy, and victorious. Undefeatable. No matter how bad a situation becomes, no matter how much opposition arises, faith knows what it has and will not be denied.

- Faith already has the answer and knows the dream cannot help but come to pass.

2. HEALINGS

Healing the sick is one of the most wonderful gifts any of us could ever have. Watching people in pain and not having any way to bring relief brings grief to anyone with a heart. God has distributed gifts that heal every sickness on earth.

The word *healings* is plural. This is because some people need emotional healing. Others need mental healing. Others need physical healing. Even within a person's "specialty" of healing there is even more specialization. Some ministers of healing have particular success with tooth problems, while others with cancers. One person ministering healing may have great faith for deafness to be healed while another has no doubt blindness will be healed. Even so, we can expect God to bring healing through us in every situation.

When we are bringing healing to people, I believe they should *not* do away with their medication. They should see their doctor. Let the doctor verify the healing. Jesus told lepers to see the priests so they could confirm their cleansing (see Luke 17:14). Healing can withstand investigation, and God is glorified.

If a person is not healed, they should *not* be told they are. Let them walk by the level of faith they have, and they will eventually receive their healing. Pretending doesn't heal anyone. Faith does! Pretending only prevents real faith from growing. When we pretend to have a bigger faith than we actually do have, we hinder real faith from rising. Honesty is part of healing too.

When people feel they are healed *they should act on it.* The minister doesn't have to throw away their medication, or crush their glasses for them. If people are healed, *let them act their own faith.* You can help them by telling them what actions they should take. Jesus told Peter to step out of the boat. He told the blind man to go wash in the pool of Siloam. Peter told the crippled beggar to stand on his feet and walk. And he did!

If people are not healed, we should *not* accuse them of sin or of not having enough faith. We may be the ones with "little" faith. Even Kathryn Kuhlman, one of Christendom's greatest healing evangelists, said she did not understand all there is to know about healing. She never tried to justify why healing didn't happen. To her, healing was a wonderful mystery. Each healing was a miracle and therefore inexplicable. We shouldn't reach conclusions about things we don't understand.

Deliverance

Sometimes people need deliverance from demons for healing to take place. Many sicknesses are the work of demons. Casting out the demon can bring healing:

And as he was still coming, the demon threw him down and convulsed him. Then Jesus rebuked the unclean spirit, healed the child, and gave him back to his father (Luke 9:42).

Then one was brought to Him who was demon-possessed, blind and mute; and He healed him, so that the blind and mute man both spoke and saw (Matthew 12:22).

Then His fame went throughout all Syria; and they brought to Him all sick people who were afflicted with various diseases and torments, and those who were demon-possessed, epileptics, and paralytics; and He healed them (Matthew 4:24).

Some sickness is the result of curses placed on people. Curses should be renounced so that healing can flow. Some people have inherited sickness from their parents or from their family line. This can also be broken by renouncing its power and claiming the family line of God Himself. *Christ has redeemed us from the curse of the law, having become a curse for us...* (Gal. 3:13).

Healing the Sick

Faith is not the only reason people receive healing. Sometimes people have no faith at all. Yet they are healed. Sometimes those praying for the sick have little faith anything will happen yet healing takes place. Some people experience sensations like a warmth in their hands when they pray. They recognize this as healing. Kenneth Hagin recognized the need for deliverance or healing, by a fire in his hands. When he laid hands on people, he would feel fire in his hands. It would remain in both hands or jump from one to the other. By this he recognized it was either sickness or a demon needing to be cast out for healing to be effective.

An elderly man visited an outreach meeting we held in a country town. I had a word of knowledge that a man with asthma was present whom God wanted to heal. The man came forward. He didn't know God, so I led him in a prayer to receive Christ. *The most important result of any supernatural ministry is the salvation of lost people.* I laid my hand on his chest and we both felt warmth flow into his body. He breathed more easily a few times and said he felt better.

The next day he built a chicken shed on his farm! He hadn't done any work for seven years because of the asthma, but he loved the work and went back to it as soon as he could. He mustered all his children and grandchildren and brought them to our meeting the next night. They took up nearly two rows of seats. The whole family came to Christ that night.

The greatest purpose of God is the salvation of men and women everywhere. Healing reveals God's compassion for the sick. Healing shows His goodness in very real terms. Healing shows His power to do what is impossible with mortals. God wants to solve people's problems and heal their sicknesses. Healing is probably the most powerful way to reveal His goodness and power.

Some diseases have their roots in attitudes or emotions. Emotional sickness will manifest somewhere in a body. Just healing the symptom does not always get rid of the problem. With the word of knowledge, discerning of spirits, and word of wisdom, we can bring complete healing to people. After we identify the root of the sickness and present that insight with wisdom, the sufferer is then able to deal with sickness in the soul as well. Forgiving others or confession of sin can also often be part of the healing process. We are spiritual doctors. With the gifts of the Spirit, we can deal with every level of human disease. We are meant to bring great joy and freedom to the world around us.

3. MIRACLES

This is one gift—miracles—that we really need to fully recover in the church. It reveals God's power to change threatening situations to good. Although we call healing a miracle, we cannot call all miracles healings. Water turning into wine is not healing. It's a miracle. This is a supernatural intervention in the normal course of events. Miracles are what we need when we're standing at the Red Sea, the armies of Egypt are behind us, the mountains to the north of us, the desert to the south of us, and sea is directly in front of us. This is when we desperately need a miracle, and not one that takes years, but immediately. Moses constantly worked with supernatural intervention. He was involved in working a host of miracles: plagues from the sky, parting the Red Sea, a rock that produced rivers of water, defeating an army by lifting up his hands, bread falling from Heaven, and tables of stone engraved with the finger of God, plus many, many more.

This gift is the least operated gift in the church today. To demonstrate the power of God we must show the world what God can do with impossible situations. Let me say again that all of the operation of the gifts is motivated by love. Jesus loved people and therefore worked miracles for them. From raising the dead to multiplying loaves and fishes, all were motivated by His compassion. Gifts of the Spirit have been given to us to work the works of Jesus.

> *Most assuredly, I say to you, he who believes in Me, the works that I do he will do also; and greater works than these he will do, because I go to My Father* (John 14:12).

Before we attempt to do more or "greater" works than Jesus, we should be at least doing just the same works: healing the sick, raising the dead, working miracles, and receiving private knowledge about people's lives in order to help them.

If we are ever to become as effective as Christ was on this earth, we cannot ignore our desperate need to move in the Holy Spirit.

Spiritual gifts are foundations of Christian life that should not be neglected—nor overestimated!

ENDNOTES

1. Martyn Lloyd-Jones, *Joy Unspeakable* (Shaw Books, 2007).

2. John Wesley, *The Journal of the Rev. John Wesley: Vol. I* (London: J. Kershaw).

3. Claude Fleury, John Wesley, George Whitefield, and Daniel

Rowland, *The Manners of the Antient Christians* (London: Felix Farley, 1749).

4. Ibid.

5. Ibid.

6. Peter Cartwright, *Backwoods Preacher* (London: Arthur Hall, Virtue and Co., 1862).

7. Charles Haddon Spurgeon, *Sermons of Rev. C.H. Spurgeon of London* (New York: Sheldon and Co., 1869).

8. William Mackelvie, William Blair, and David Young, *Annals and Statistics of the United Presbyterian Church* (Edinburgh: Oliphant & Co., 1873).

FOUNDATION FIVE

Laying on of Hands

IF IT HAD BEEN UP to me to put together the seven vital truths essential for a foundation in Christ, I would not have even considered the laying on of hands. Yet, over the years it is obvious that one of the first things that empowers a new Christian is the laying on of hands.

In our worship services at C3 Church, we regularly include altar calls in which people can receive impartation. Everyone must grow; and dependency upon this ministry brings growth in early stages. As believers grow and learn to stand on their own feet, their need for spiritual impartation from others decreases. They develop a far more self-sufficient Christian lifestyle.

The laying on of hands signifies impartation, transference, transmission, and identification. The practice takes place throughout the Bible—in both the Old and New Testaments—and under diverse circumstances. Let's look at seven of these circumstances.

1. IMPARTING BLESSING

> *Then Israel stretched out his right hand and laid it upon Ephraim's head, who was the younger, and his left hand on Manasseh's head, guiding his hands knowingly…* (Genesis 48:14).

The anointing is *imparted* through laying on of hands. In Genesis 48:18, Israel blesses Joseph's sons Manasseh and Ephraim, placing his hands on them. He deliberately lays his right hand on Ephraim. He wants greater blessing for him. A greater anointing flows through one hand than the other. We must understand that the Holy Spirit guides us. As we follow Him, the touch of God flows. Joseph wanted the greater blessing to come upon Manasseh, his firstborn. However, Jacob would not allow this, as he was being guided by the Lord. The greater blessing was to fall upon Ephraim. Thus, he used his right hand. This indicated that there is not only significance in the laying on of hands but also in how it is done.

2. TRANSMISSION

> *Then he shall put his hand on the head of the burnt offering and it will be accepted on his behalf to make atonement for him* (Leviticus 1:4).

This Scripture passage from Leviticus signifies that God recognizes the transmission of sin through the laying on of hands. The animal was thus considered a substitute offering for the offerer. This is called an "atoning sacrifice"; the animal died in his place, after hands were laid on its head.

A definite transmission takes place through the laying on of hands. In the New Testament, however, the transmission of sin does not come into play, because Christ has become our once for all sacrifice. Our sins have been transmitted to Him once for all. He has died in our place.

3. IMPARTATION OF SPIRITUAL BENEFITS AND GIFTS

Now Joshua the son of Nun was full of the spirit of wisdom, for Moses had laid his hands on him; so the children of Israel heeded him… (Deuteronomy 34:9).

The same wisdom that had resided in Moses now is in Joshua. This has been "imparted" to Joshua through Moses laying his hands on the man. The entire nation of Israel recognized that this had taken place, and so the children of Israel heeded Moses.

New Testament ministers use this method to impart supernatural ability just like Paul imparted a spiritual gift to Timothy through the laying on of hands: *"…the gift of God which is in you through the laying on of hands"* (2 Tim. 1:6) and *"the gift that is in you, which is given to you by prophecy with the laying on of the hands of the eldership"* (1 Tim. 4:14), display that when we lay hands on a person with the intention to impart, spiritual life is transmitted.

Men and women with authority in the Kingdom of God are able to impart their own spiritual gifts into the lives of those under them. This happens through the laying on of hands.

4. HEALING THE SICK

The healing power of God is also transmitted by believers through the laying on of hands. Jesus healed in this way, too: *…He laid His hands on every one of them and healed them* (Luke 4:40).

Jesus healed the sick and cast out demons through the laying on of hands. In fact, the very next verse exclaims, *"demons also came out of many"* (Luke 4:41).

Believers are told by Christ to lay their hands on the sick for their recovery: *...they will lay hands on the sick and they will recover* (Mark 16:18).

James also exhorted believers to pray one for another that we might be healed (see James 5:16). Here too, the practice of laying on of hands is to be used so that healing will flow throughout the Body of Christ through the believers themselves.

5. BAPTISM OF THE HOLY SPIRIT

The empowerment of believers with the Holy Spirit takes place through the laying on of hands. At the start, the apostles received this experience directly from Heaven in the Upper Room without anyone laying hands on anyone else. Yet, when they came to impart the experience to other new Christians, they used the laying on of hands: *...Then they laid hands on them and they received the Holy Spirit* (Acts 8:14-17).

6. APPOINTMENT OF CHURCH OFFICERS

whom they set before the Apostles; and when they had prayed, they laid hands on them (Acts 6:6).

The men referred to in Acts 6:6 (Stephen, Philip, Procorus, Nicanor, Timon, Parmenas, and Nicolas) were appointed as deacons to handle the practical affairs of the early church. Once they had been selected, the apostles laid their hands on them, empowering them for service in the Kingdom of God.

7. RELEASING OF MINISTRIES

When Paul and Barnabas were sent out on the first missionary journey, the ministers at the church in Antioch came together to pray. As they sought the Lord together, the Holy Spirit indicated that these two men were to be separated for a task He had already spoken to them about.

> *Then, having fasted and prayed, and laid hands on them, they sent them away. So, being sent out by the Holy Spirit, they went...* (Acts 13:3-4).

Thus the Great Commission of Christ began to be fulfilled.

FOUNDATION SIX

—

Resurrection of the Dead

ONE-THIRD OF THE FOUNDATION OF the Christian life has to do with the unseen, invisible future. It is presented with a mixed attitude of hope and sober responsibility: resurrection and judgment. The two subjects are inextricably linked and have to do with the ultimate purpose of God in salvation.

The Greek word for "resurrection" is *anastsis*, which means "to stand up" (*ana*, "up"; and *histemi*, "to cause to stand") [1]. The resurrection is the great hope of the believer. Apostle Paul is desperate to be included in this awesome event:

> *I count all things loss for the excellence of the knowledge of Christ Jesus my Lord…that I may know Him and the power of His resurrection…if by any means I might attain to the resurrection from the dead* (Philippians 3:8;10-11).

Paul goes on to say that if Christ is not risen, then *"we are of all men the most pitiable"* (1 Cor. 15:16-19).

Before we view the resurrection, however, it is vital that we understand what occurs at, and after, death. According to Ecclesiastes 12:7, when a person dies, the dust returns to the ground it came from and the spirit returns to God. When Jesus died, He cried out to God, *"into Your hands I commit My spirit"* (Luke 23:46). Thus, God appoints a place of waiting to those disembodied spirits. They await the day of resurrection and then judgment. Everyone will be resurrected. No one is exempt.

> *Do not marvel at this; for the hour is coming in which all who are in the graves will hear His voice and come forth; those who have done good, to the resurrection of life, and those who have done evil to the resurrection of condemnation* (John 5:28-29).

We will each be examined as to how we have lived our lives. For the Christian, judgment passes the moment they receive Christ. However, the unbeliever will be judged at the end of time. (We will look more closely at those subjects in the last foundational truth—Eternal Judgment.)

I believe that after a believer dies, he is assigned to wait in Paradise, as Jesus told the thief who was hung on a cross beside Him: *Assuredly, I say to you, today, you shall be with Me in Paradise* (Luke 23:43).

And if a person is not saved when they die, then they are assigned to hades: ... *The rich man also died and was buried. And being in torments in Hades...* (Luke 16:22-23).

After we die, even though we are not in possession of a physical body, we still have all the sensing faculties of a body. It would seem that a "spirit" person exists who possesses all the abilities of the "physical" person.

In Luke 16:19-31 we discover the story of Lazarus and the rich man. Jesus clearly describes the state of people after they are dead. This story is not a parable (never does Jesus employ personal names in the telling of parables); neither does the context describe this story as a parable. When Jesus spoke in parables, the writer announces them as such. The recounting of Luke 16:19, however, is a specific teaching on realities of the afterlife.

Paradise (what most Christians call "Heaven") is also referred to as "Abraham's bosom." This indicates that it is a place of comfort. The rich man is "in torments," yet he is able to see. He *"lifted up his eyes and saw Abraham afar off, and Lazarus..."* (Luke 16:23). The rich man feels the heat and suffers from undying thirst. He communicates with Abraham. He requests just a small amount of water to cool his tongue. Abraham tells him to "remember" his life on earth. This indicates that after death we are able to recall our life on earth, including recognizing people we knew when we were on earth.

Abraham reveals to the rich man that there is an impassable gulf between Paradise and hades and that none are able to traverse it. The rich man remembers his family on earth and pleads with Abraham to send Lazarus to them so they will believe and not arrive in hades. This tells us that we are therefore capable also of feeling emotional ties with earth—compassion, desperation, concern, etc. No consciousness is lost after death. Rather, it would seem that we are heightened to a full comprehension of external realities. (Isaiah 14 and Ezekiel 32 also reveal some of the conditions that exist after death.)

As quickly as a believer dies, they are in the presence of God: *Absent from the body...present with the Lord* (2 Cor. 5:8).

No matter what destruction happened to our body at death or since death, we will be reconstructed fully to appear before God, body, soul, and spirit. He is well able to do this, as the Psalmist says: *...and in Thy book all my members were written...* (Ps. 139:16 KJV).

God knows how He put you together. He is well aware of colors and sizes. Even then, it is certain that changes for the better will take place. When Christ rose from the dead, He was unrecognizable to the disciples: *...Jesus Himself drew near and went with them. But their eyes were restrained, so that they did not know Him* (Luke 24:15-16). *...she turned around and saw Jesus standing there, and did not know that it was Jesus* (John 20:14).

While there will be distinct differences between our resurrection and the Lord's, the Bible says we shall be like Him!

> *...it has not yet been revealed what we shall be, but we know that when He is revealed, we shall be like Him, for we shall see Him as He is* (1 John 3:2).

THREE PARTS, ONE PERSON

It is important to understand that we are made up of three areas—a spirit, a soul, and a body:

> *...may your whole spirit, soul, and body be preserved blameless at the coming of our Lord Jesus Christ...* (1 Thessalonians 5:23-24).

When we initially receive Christ we are born again. That is, we receive a new spirit, as God said through the prophet Ezekiel: *I will... put a new spirit within you...My Spirit within you...* (Ezek. 36:26-27).

At the point of receiving Christ and becoming born again, our *spirit* is a recipient of the resurrection power of Christ. It is completely saved and made to be right with God. It is in perfect harmony with Him; it bears His image of God; it has eternal life.

But our *soul* enters into a process of "being" saved. Our spirit is the intuitive, knowing part of our makeup. It's the part that gets inspiration and revelation from God. It has a spirit consciousness. The spirit is that part of us that motivates us. It worships God. It is through our spirit that God communicates with us. However, our soul is the seat of our inner self—the emotions, the attitudes, the conscience, the personality, the character, the mind. This part of our makeup is being worked on constantly by God to conform us to the image of Jesus:

> *But we all, with unveiled face, beholding as in a mirror the glory of the Lord, are being transformed into the same image from glory to glory, just as by the Spirit of the Lord* (2 Corinthians 3:18).

As mentioned previously, the inner self is comprised of spirit and soul "welded" together. In other words, our soul is infused with our spirit. Thus, our soul is also eternal; our self-conscious soul lives on after death.

On the other hand, our bodies are not yet saved at all. Occasionally they may be healed supernaturally and sustained by the power of God when needed, but basically they yet await their "redemption."

ASSURANCE OF BODILY RESURRECTION

The assurance that the bodily resurrection part of our salvation will take place is given through the presence of the Holy Spirit in us. He is called the *seal of our redemption* (see Eph. 1:13-14). The word *seal* literally means to make an impression. This would be akin to a king's signet ring pressed into hot wax, indicating His authority, ownership, and authentication. The Holy Spirit is the seal of redemption to the believer with regard to God's promise of the resurrection.

Certainly the receiving of the Holy Spirit is a powerful event, resulting in effective service for Christ, but it also includes the giving of assurance regarding the resurrection. It is the raising of the body. It happens supernaturally the moment we repent and receive Christ.

RESURRECTION *NOW* GUARANTEES RESURRECTION *THEN*

Most assuredly, I say to you, the hour is coming and now is, when the dead will hear the voice of the Son of God, and those who hear will live (John 5:25).

In this Scripture passage from John 5, Jesus reveals that if we hear the voice of the Son of God now, here on earth, then we will receive a spiritual resurrection right now. This in turn guarantees that we will hear His voice in that "hour" when the *"dead shall hear His voice and come forth to everlasting life"* (John 5:24). At this point, our "whole" body, soul, and spirit as one complete unit will be united to stand before God. Thus, the resurrection of the dead deals mainly with the physical body.

BUT WHEN?

When does all this take place? The answer is, around the time of the end. In other words, at the Second Coming of Christ:

> *For the Lord Himself will descend from heaven with a shout, with the voice of an archangel, and with the trumpet of God. And the dead in Christ will rise first. Then we who are alive and remain shall be caught up together with them in the clouds to meet the Lord in the air...* (1 Thessalonians 4:16-17).

The timing of "the rapture" is concurrent with the descent of Jesus from Heaven at His Second Coming.

There are a thousand and one different views on the subject of the Second Coming. Without being too casual regarding this subject, we will deal only with the major points of the event.

When we look back over the history of God's people and His dealings with them, we find that there are a few very significant details regarding this all-important event. For every prophecy telling us that there was to be a First Coming of Christ, there are at least four others telling us He is coming again. Therefore, we can be four times as sure of His Second Coming as of His first—and we all know He was here the first time. However, above all of the differences of opinion regarding the Second Coming, we must keep this one fact firmly in place: *Christ is coming again.*

THE PURPOSE OF PROPHECY

One of the problems in biblical prophecy is knowing how we are meant to use it. The prophet Daniel was motivated by the prophecy of Jeremiah concerning the return of the Jews to Jerusalem after seventy years in Babylon. He realized that the seventy years were almost completed at the time he read the prophecy. His response was to begin to pray:

> *...I, Daniel, understood by the books the number of the years specified by the word of the Lord through Jeremiah the prophet, that He would accomplish seventy years in the desolations of Jerusalem. Then I set my face toward the Lord God to make request by prayer and supplications, with fasting, sackcloth, and ashes* (Daniel 9:2-3).

King Cyrus of Persia was then prompted to act just as the prophet Isaiah had spoken of him:

> *Thus says Cyrus king of Persia: All the kingdoms of the earth the Lord God of heaven has given me. And He has commanded me to build Him a house at Jerusalem...* (Ezra 1:2).

> *...Cyrus... is My shepherd, and he shall perform all My pleasure, saying to Jerusalem, "You shall be built," and to the temple, "Your foundation shall be laid"* (Isaiah 44:28).

There are many more instances throughout Scripture where men were motivated by prophecy to act for God.

PROPHECY MOTIVATES PREPAREDNESS

When we come to the prophecies regarding the Second Coming of Christ, our actions are to be summed up as *"Be ready!" Therefore you also be ready, for the Son of Man is coming at an hour you do not expect* (Luke 12:40).

Again and again, Jesus repeats the message "Be ready." Equally as consistent is His reason for saying this: because we do not know the hour or the day when He will return.

Many Christians have fallen into error when they have disagreed with Scripture and attempted to tell us the exact timing of the Second Coming. But not even Jesus Himself is aware of that day and hour: *But of that day and hour no one knows, not even the angels of heaven, but My Father only* (Matt. 24:36).

Human nature is such that if we were aware of the timing of when Jesus is returning, we would arrange to get right before God at that moment, rather than well in advance. The thought that Christ could come at any time is a powerful motivator for us to live right.

> *...when He is revealed, we shall be like Him, for we shall see Him as He is. And everyone who has this hope in Him purifies himself, just as He is pure* (1 John 3:2-3).

> *Therefore, beloved, looking forward to these things, be diligent to be found by Him in peace, without spot and blameless* (2 Peter 3:14).

The rapture is the event when the bodies of believers will be changed in the *"twinkling of an eye"* (1 Cor. 15:52) and then be caught up, off the earth, in a massive translation of believers from this planet into Heaven.

DANIEL'S 70 WEEKS

Daniel prophesied of a seventy-year period when Israel would be dealt with in a specific way:

> *Seventy weeks are determined for your people and for your holy city...from the going forth of the command to restore and build Jerusalem until Messiah the Prince, there shall be seven weeks and sixty-two weeks; the street shall be built again, and*

the wall, even in troublesome times. And after the sixty-two weeks Messiah shall be cut off, but not for Himself; and the people of the prince who is to come shall destroy the city and the sanctuary. The end of it shall be with a flood, and till the end of the war desolations are determined. Then he shall confirm a covenant with many for one week; but in the middle of the week He shall bring an end to sacrifice and offering. And on the wing of abominations shall be one who makes desolate... (Daniel 9:24-27).

With regard to these seventy weeks (or "seventy sevens of years"), each day of each week represents one year (seven days times seventy years), which totals a period of 490 years (of which Bible scholars and commentators are in agreement). Per Daniel 9:2, the prophet was in prayer concerning years, not weeks. It is obvious that sixty-nine weeks have already been accomplished; but it is the final seventieth week where many different opinions arise. Some believe that it is still in the future;[2] others believe it has already passed. However, it is not inconceivable that prophecy can have double, even multiple, fulfillments.[3]

MULTIPLE FULFILLMENT OF SCRIPTURE

In the Isaiah chapter 14 description of the fall of lucifer, the message is also directed at the king of Babylon. The same applies to Ezekiel 26 in the prophet's denunciation of the king of Tyre. Thus, Daniel may have been covering more than a single circumstance in his prophecy.

THE HISTORICAL VIEW

History tells us that a "Messiah" has come (Jesus) and that He declared that He was *"not sent except to the lost sheep of the house of Israel"*

(Matt. 15:24). Jesus makes this statement after a Canaanite woman approached Him for the healing of her daughter. Initially Jesus refuses to respond to her. But after His disciples beseech Him to send her away because she is so insistently pleading with Him, He tells them that He *"was not sent except to the lost sheep of the house of Israel."* Essentially, Jesus was objecting to the woman's request on the grounds that the powers He has are reserved for the house of Israel (something Jesus had similarly instructed His disciples in Matthew 10:5-6 when He said, *"do not enter a city of the Samaritans, but go rather to the lost sheep of the House of Israel"*).

The earthly ministry of Christ lasted for approximately three and a half years. After the birthing of the Church on the day of Pentecost, it was approximately another three and a half years to the stoning of Stephen—at which point the Church scattered from Jerusalem to the "ends of the earth." Up until this point, the Church had been reaching out to and touching only the Jewish community and those who were proselytes to the Jewish faith. Now, however, the Gospel was being preached in Samaria, Caesarea, and as far away as Rome—with tremendous impact.

It is therefore not unreasonable to deduce that the seventieth week of Daniel could have been fulfilled in this time when Messiah was "cut off," in the middle of the week, causing the offering to cease, and thus breaking the (Old Testament) covenant. Jesus caused all the Old Testament requirements of offerings to cease, having fulfilled them Himself in His one-time offering for sin "once for all." He also inaugurated a new Covenant (that is, the New Testament), doing away with the Old.

If we take this interpretation onboard, much of what some teachers say has not yet come to pass has actually already taken place. This means the Second Coming could be much more imminent than we think—like *today*. This is definitely the perception that Christ wanted to project, so believers would be always ready and anticipating His imminent return.

THE FUTURIST VIEW

People who believe there is yet a remaining seven-year period of time need to see a host of things take place before the Second Coming occurs. To say that God has not been fulfilling any prophecies in previous centuries but only during our own is somewhat egocentric. However, there are definite signs that indicate the fulfillment of prophecies in our lifetimes.

The futurist point of view is called "pre-millennial," which means they believe the Second Coming will happen prior to the Millennium, which is the thousand-year reign of Christ spoken of by the aged apostle John: *...And they lived and reigned with Christ for a thousand years* (Rev. 20:4).

DIFFERENT VIEWS

There are several different views about when the saints will be raptured (translated) and when the Second Coming will take place. Most pre-millennialists, however, agree that there will be a one-world ruler known as the antichrist (mentioned as such in First and Second John). He will be accompanied by a "false prophet" and "the beast." Some say that both events will be simultaneous. As Christ makes His public appearance for the second time to planet Earth, the Church will be "caught up" to meet Him in the air. These theorists argue that God will allow His Church to pass through the "great tribulation" spoken of by the apostle John: *... These are the ones who come out of the great tribulation...* (Rev. 7:14).

This point of view holds that God will not spare His people from the tribulation. This is comparable to the circumstances of the early Christians under the persecution of Rome, as well as Christians suffering intense persecutions throughout history.

A "SECRET COMING" VIEW

Possibly the most publicized (and seemingly most popular) concept today among Spirit-filled groups is that the rapture will take place at a "secret" coming of Christ prior to the seven-year period when God will deal specifically with Israel. The basis for this thought is that the Church needs to be removed so that it is no longer the focus of God's dealings in the earth. The theory is that God's people will be removed from the great tribulation just as Noah and his family were saved from the judgment of God in the earth, so that the hindering influence of the Church against the antichrist is removed. This would effectively release all manner of evil on the earth.

It is believed that at this time the believers will attend the marriage supper of the Lamb and receive their rewards at the judgment seat of Christ. Just prior to this time, it is believed that a series of events will take place that will set the stage for the antichrist to assume a one-world rulership.

The major points:

1. Financial Collapse

A worldwide financial collapse concurrent with a new trading system. This will mean receiving a mark on the back of the hand or on the forehead thus enabling people to trade. Receiving this mark will also somehow signify allegiance to, and worship of, the beast or the new one-world ruler.

2. A New Roman Empire

A revived Roman Empire of ten nations emerging out of a European unification. They will be the initial platform for the world ruler. They will unite as one under this ruler. They will give him the authority to lead them. This corresponds to the ten toes of the vision of Daniel 2:41-42:

> *Whereas you saw the feet and toes, partly of potter's clay and partly of iron, the kingdom shall be divided; yet the strength of the iron shall be in it, just as you saw the iron mixed with ceramic clay. And as the toes of the feet were partly of iron and partly of clay, so the kingdom shall be partly strong and partly fragile.*

3. Temporary Peace in the Middle East

The antichrist will bring peace to the Middle East situation through a contract. However, the terms of this contract will be broken after three and a half years. Also, he will ignore the nations who initially gave him the power and assume the role of a dictator. After this, the great tribulation will ensue, with many atrocities.

It seems that many of these things are already taking place in the world today. It is very conceivable that such prophecies are right now beginning to come to reality.

FLEXIBILITY IN INTERPRETATION FOR WISDOM'S SAKE

By discussing these various viewpoints, my intention is not to confuse. Rather, I would prefer that we retain a flexibility in our interpretation of prophecy. When we become rigid, we make the Gospel and her messengers appear foolish (as so many Christians have done). This only deepens resistance to the Gospel and to Christianity in general. We must walk with wisdom.

However, the one issue on which we have no room for compromise or negotiation is the fact that Jesus Christ is returning to Earth to take home all those who have received Him!

THE MAIN EVENTS

At the resurrection of the dead, the bodies of the dead are raised out of the graves, while the bodies of the living are transformed. In his letter to the Thessalonians, apostle Paul gives an overview of this wondrous occurrence:

> *For the Lord Himself will descend from Heaven with a shout, with the voice of an archangel and with the trumpet of God and the dead in Christ will rise first. Then we who are alive and remain shall be caught up together with them in the clouds to meet the Lord in the air. And thus we shall always be with the Lord* (1 Thessalonians 4:16-17).

The main events that comprise the Second Coming of Christ Messiah:

1. **Jesus Calling His Saints**. *"…the hour is coming in which all who are in the graves will hear His voice and come forth…"* (John 5:28-29).

2. **Voice of the Archangel**. *"…with the voice of an archangel…"* (1 Thessalonians 4:16).

3. **Trumpet of God**. *"...with the trumpet of God..."* (1 Thessalonians 4:16).

4. **The Saints Resurrected**. The resurrection of the saints from the graves and the translation of those who are alive. There is a resurrection order described in First Corinthians 15:22-23: *"...in Christ all shall be made alive. But each one in his own order: Christ the firstfruits, afterward those who are Christ's at His coming."*

OLD TESTAMENT SAINTS

The first group to receive the resurrection body was the Old Testament saints who rose at the time of the death and resurrection of Jesus. These are the "first fruits" mentioned by Matthew:

and the graves were opened and many bodies of the saints who had fallen asleep were raised; and coming out of the graves after His resurrection, they went into the holy city and appeared to many (Matthew 27:52-53).

These Old Testament saints received their new body and walked about the streets before ascending with Jesus into Heaven. In Hebrews 12:1 we are told that we are *"surrounded by a great cloud of witnesses."* These are the ancient heroes of faith. We are also told that Jesus was received up into a cloud as He ascended from Earth. This could very well have been that same cloud of the Old Testament personalities who rose with Jesus into Heaven as He went to take His seat at the right hand of the throne of God.

THOSE IN CHRIST AT HIS COMING

The next in the order is "those who are Christ's at His Coming." This includes us! Paul anticipates the question of some to be, "With what body?" (see 1 Cor. 15:35). Our bodies will be transformed in a moment of time. Paul uses the analogy of a seed of corn being sown in the ground. Obviously something different emerges from the soil after a period of time. Something much more fruitful, glorious, amazing, and useful. To Paul, death was like sowing a seed.

The first person to ever receive the resurrection body was Jesus Christ. What this body is made of and how it functions is something of a mystery. However, from the post-resurrection appearances of Jesus, some things are evident:

- The resurrected body does not appear to be gravity bound, but seems to have the capacity to lift off from Earth (see Acts 1 and Rev. 11).

- This body seems to be able to pass through walls. When Jesus appeared to the disciples after He was crucified and before He ascended to Heaven, Scripture notes that Jesus entered the room, though the doors were closed and locked (see John 20:19 and 26).

- The resurrected body can be touched by those who have bodies of flesh (it's not like vapor or a "ghost"), because Jesus asked Thomas to feel His wounds, which had been caused by the nails (see John 20:27).

- This body can eat food. Jesus ate fish with the two men he accompanied walking to Emmaus (see Luke 24:41-43). So, eating remains part of our lives as the resurrected.

- The new body can become invisible or visible at will. Jesus disappeared from the Emmaus disciples (see Luke 24:31).

First Corinthians 15:42-44 lists five major changes that will take place at the bodily resurrection:

1. **Corruption to Incorruptible**: No decay will accompany this new body. It will remain eternally vigorous, healthy, and youthful. This means it passes from being mortal to immortal. It will never die. Death has no power whatsoever over this new body. It cannot be corrupted.

2. **Dishonor to Glory**: Imperfections, frequent ailments, and injuries often cause humiliation and embarrassment. In J.B. Phillips' *The New Testament in Modern English*, apostle Paul declares that of all this will change, and we will have a body of "splendor."

3. **Weakness to Power**: All deficiencies in power, strength, stamina, and energy will be gone. That is a powerful body. What we possess now is weak compared to that which awaits the saved. Paul had caught a clear vision of this new world and our physical state in it. His vision of the gloriousness of it all paints our present circumstances with a drab brush.

4. **Natural to Spiritual**: The substance of this new body is different from flesh. It endures for eternity. It is spirit. It can enter Heaven. It has the faculties to function as a spirit in the spirit world. Yet it would seem that it is not just a spirit. We see Jesus doing things that a spirit cannot do. Paul also explains that although we will all be raised in "glory," there will be differing orders of glory. Some will be more glorious than others.

5. **Flesh and Blood to Light**: The prophet Daniel says, *"many of those who sleep in the dust...shall awake... Those who are wise shall shine like the brightness of the firmament, and those who turn many to righteousness like the stars forever and ever"* (Dan. 12:2-3). This also confirms the word that God spoke to Abraham thousands of years earlier: *"count the stars if you are able to number them...so shall your descendants be"* (Gen. 15:5). By New Testament definition, we are considered to be the descendants of Abraham (see Gal. 3:7). These two Scriptures then tell us that we will literally glow with the glory of God. However, some will own more glory than others. This, I imagine, may be part of the rewards of Heaven. First Corinthians 15:41-42 says, *"There is one glory of the sun, another glory of the moon, and another glory of the stars; for one star differs from another star in glory. So also is the resurrection of the dead...."* Could this mean that "light" will be our energy source, rather than blood? After all, John 1:4 says, *"In Him was life, and the life was the light of men."*

As there is a different kind of flesh for all creatures and species of creatures on the earth and in Heaven, so too is the resurrection body a new kind of "flesh."

HEAVEN: OUR FUTURE HOME

Our future home in Heaven is described in Revelation 21. From the description given, we can ascertain that it is approximately 1,500 miles long by 1,500 miles wide by 1,500 miles high. It hangs in space and its appearance from a distance is shimmering green—"jasper." Heaven could be the shape of a cube or a pyramid. The enormous wall surrounding it is made of all manner of precious stones, so that it glows and sparkles with the light of God's glory. On this four-wall pyramid, each of the four walls contains three gates made of a pearl-like substance. The basic material of Heaven is a transparent gold. There is no need of sun, moon, or any other lighting, for the glory of God lights the entire place. Heaven could be a planet on which this city, the New Jerusalem, is found. Or it could be that the various names all refer to the same place. Whatever its appearance, it is our future abode.

In my Father's house are many mansions: if it were not so I would have told you. I go to prepare a place for you. And if I go and prepare a place for you, I will come again and receive you to Myself; that where I am, there you may be also (John 14:2-3).

That is the ultimate purpose of Christ, to go and prepare a place for us—those who have joined themselves to Him. He then returns to earth and collects those same ones who are His, to receive them into Heaven so that we may be where He is forever and ever.

Because of Christ's resurrection, death no longer reigns. We do! We have health instead of sickness. Life instead of death. Light instead of darkness. Wealth instead of poverty. And we have solutions for the problems people face. There is no problem for which God has not already provided the answer. There is no problem any of us face that is bigger than the God inside us. There is no problem humankind faces that cannot be solved through the complete salvation of the cross of Christ!

ENDNOTES

1. *Strong's Dictionary*, #G386.

2. Chronologically, these "weeks of years" started in 445 B.C. when King Artaxerxes commanded that Jerusalem be restored. Thus, the 490 years could be divided as such: *Seven Sevens* = 49 years; from 445-396 B.C. from Artaxerxes' decree to the arrival of Nehemiah and the covenant renewal celebration at Jerusalem. *Sixty-two Sevens* = 434 years; 396 B.C. to A.D. 32 (from the dedication of the second temple to the crucifixion of Christ). Under this scenario, the *Final Seven* = unfulfilled; but the interpretation is that national Israel will make a pact with the future "one who makes desolate" (the antichrist, the Roman prince of Daniel 11:8 and 11:36) for seven years—this seventieth week. In the middle of this final seven-year period, the antichrist will break the pact and demand that the blood sacrifices restored by Israel in the last days shall cease. Antichrist will set up his image in the Jewish temple and require that he be worshiped.

3. In fact, one interpretation of Daniel 9:24-27 views the numerical computation of the previous footnote as purely subjective, while others take a multilevel approach to fulfillment of this prophecy.

FOUNDATION SEVEN

Eternal Judgment

THE SEVENTH AND FINAL ELEMENT of the foundation to be laid for the Christian is the revelation of the judgment of God.

FEAR OF GOD

The fear of God is crucial to a successful Christian life. Not all fear is bad. Said another way, the fear of God is good. At the consummation of all the searching of Solomon for the ultimate purpose of life he concluded:

> *Let us hear the conclusion of the whole matter:* **Fear God** *and keep His commandments: for this is the whole duty of man. For God shall bring every work into judgment with every secret thing, whether it be good or whether it be bad* (Ecclesiastes 12:13-14 NIV).

The fear of God has its roots in knowing that God is a Judge who will one day pass judgment and sentence on every life born on this planet.

Why would God want us to fear Him? Primarily because it modifies our behavior. So we please God!

…by the fear of the Lord one departs from evil (Proverbs 16:6).

Therefore, having these promises, beloved, let us cleanse ourselves from all filthiness of the flesh and spirit, perfecting holiness in the fear of God (2 Corinthians 7:1).

The fear of the Lord is the beginning of wisdom… (Proverbs 9:10).

It seems incompatible that we are required to fear God, yet to love Him with all our hearts. But these two very spiritual emotions are able to synthesize within us to produce both a perfect love and a perfect fear for God.

HELL

Another seeming anomaly that the natural mind has difficulty reconciling is that a God who "is love" has also created a hell where humans will spend eternity as judgment.

As we read Scripture, we also see the judgment of God falling upon people when they rebelled against Him. This is not exclusive to the Old Testament, either. The judgment of God is just as much a New Testament reality. The answer is not to compromise Scripture just because it isn't convenient for us to perceive God as Judge in this generation.

Some of us can feel somewhat embarrassed by the fact that terrible things do happen resulting from the judgment of God. We can attempt to soften the truth of judgment with reasoning that we would never apply to other more "positive" Scripture. The plain facts are that God judges sin, chastises His children, and will call all to account for our behavior at the Last Day. The reality of that day must be driven well home into our hearts. We cannot just live however we want and hope to get away with it. God has laid down His requirements for us. When we fail to respond, we suffer the consequences. The same justice that condemns, also saves!

True justice is impartial and fair. Therefore, when it is just to reward one for obedience, then it is just to recompense for disobedience. In fact, it is against this backdrop that salvation is most clearly seen. We may imagine that salvation is deliverance from sickness and earthly troubles, and the gift of eternal life; but salvation is also preservation from the final and all-consuming judgment of God. At the judgment of the wicked, they are cast into hell.

The judgment we are speaking of here is that which belongs to the end of the age. The judgments of God are in the earth today; however, the writer of Hebrews is referring to those judgments that affect our position in eternity: *You have come to God, the judge of all men…* (Heb. 12:23 NIV).

Even though God enforces the penalties for breaches of His law, it is neither His desire nor pleasure to carry out these acts:

> *The Lord is not slack concerning His promise, as some count slackness, but is longsuffering toward us, not willing that any should perish but that all should come to repentance* (2 Peter 3:9).

Some perceive that because the Lord has taken so long to return, this is a reason to doubt that He ever will. This is actually a demonstration of the longsuffering of God. He is not in any rush for the Day of Judgment. He would far prefer that all would repent and escape that day. Thus, He lingers longer, hoping the Church will do its great work and for people throughout the world to respond positively to the Gospel. Without exception, all persons will be judged:

> *For we must all appear before the judgment seat of Christ...* (2 Corinthians 5:10).

The reason Christ came was not for judgment, but salvation:

> *For God did not send His Son into the world to condemn the world, but that the world through Him might be saved* (John 3:17).

It has never been the intention of God to send humankind to hell:

> *Then He will say to those on His left hand, "Depart from Me, you cursed, into the everlasting fire prepared for the devil and his angels"* (Matthew 25:41).

Unfortunately, man has aligned himself with satan, the archenemy of God, and thus has inherited the same destiny. Hell was not prepared for humankind. It was not the intention of the Creator that His children would burn forever in hell as the devil would. But now we have only two choices: we can be children of the devil or children of God. Eternity will be spent with whoever we align ourselves with here on earth.

It is clear that it is God's ultimate joy to bring salvation and mercy to all of humanity. He is reluctant to bring wrath and judgment.

FOUR MAIN GUIDING PRINCIPLES OF JUDGMENT

There are four main guiding principles of divine judgment found in Romans:

> *But we know that the judgment of God is according to truth...*
> *who will render to each one according to his deeds...there is no*
> *partiality with God. For as many as have sinned without the*
> *law will also perish without law, and as many as have sinned in*
> *the law will be judged by the law...* (Romans 2:2,6,11-12).

1. TRUTH

Only God knows what ultimate truth is in any given situation. He alone is able to correctly scrutinize each person's life and weigh it correctly against Heaven's requirements and earth's surrounding circumstances. Truth is the combination of love and judgment, mercy, and rewards. It is God's recognition of the degree of responsibility each person had for their actions.

2. DEEDS

We will be judged according to our works. Even though we are not saved by works, we will be judged by them. Salvation must be accompanied with acts that reveal the presence of God in us. Sometimes we hear the statement that "at least he has a good heart." Generally, this is an attempt to atone for that person's failings. However, we will not be judged, whether we are Christian or non-Christian, by our attitude or whether or not we have a good heart, but by our works. Luke 6:44 says, *"every tree is known by its own fruit."* Thus, God judges us by our works, those things we have actually done. We are not going to be judged by intentions, attitudes, hopes, visions, or even by gifts or talents. Our deeds are the final revelation of who we are and what our character is.

3. NO PARTIALITY

Without partiality means that God will not take into account whether people are rich or poor, educated or not, kings or paupers. For the purpose of judgment, a person's earthly state will count for nothing. We will stand naked of all these things before the Lord.

4. MORAL LIGHT WITHIN

Often we are asked as to how those who have never heard the Gospel will be judged. Here is the answer: according to the amount of moral light within each person. Only God can measure such a thing. But if people have lived in that light, then they will be judged accordingly. If they have disobeyed what they have known to be correct, then the same applies. Obviously this is difficult to do since the flesh has little power to resist its own impulses and appetite for evil. Thus, it is upon us to do all we can to obey the great commission. We must carry salvation to the ends of the earth.

THREE MAIN SCENES OF JUDGMENT

There are three main scenes of judgment at the end of the age: The Judgment Seat of Christ, The Throne of Christ's Glory, and The Great White Throne of Judgment.

Before we discuss these three main scenes, we must establish the fact that the judgment of Christians is for rewards and has nothing to do with eternal status—that is finalized when we receive Christ. He is the propitiation for our sins. The cross has totally satisfied all the punishments and penalties the justice of God demanded. According to both the Old and New Testaments, Christ bore the punishment for our sins. He stood in the way and took the punishment for our sins. He has paid the debt to the justice of God, which we could not pay:

> *He was wounded for our transgressions, He was bruised for our iniquities; the chastisement for our peace was upon Him, and by His stripes we are healed* (Isaiah 53:5).

> *Most assuredly I say to you he who hears My word and believes in Him who sent Me has everlasting life, and shall not come into judgment, but has passed from death into life* (John 5:24).

When believers are resurrected at the end of this age and prior to the millennium, we will all appear before a judgment throne. This is different from the judgment of the wicked at the end of the millennium.

> *Do not marvel at this; for the hour is coming in which all who are in the graves will hear His voice, and come forth—those who have done good to the resurrection of life, and those who have done evil to the resurrection of condemnation* (John 5:28-29).

Let's take a look at each of the three scenes of judgment.

SCENE ONE: THE JUDGMENT SEAT OF CHRIST

The Judgment Seat of Christ is where only believers will appear. This is our first step entering eternity. This judgment determines what rewards are given to who, and this also involves a final purging:

> *Now if anyone builds on this foundation with gold, silver, precious stones, wood, hay, straw, each one's work will become clear; for the Day will declare it, because it will be revealed by fire; and the fire will test each one's work, what sort it is. If anyone's work which he has built on it endures, he will receive a reward. If anyone's work*

is burned he will suffer loss; but he himself will be saved, yet so as through fire (1 Corinthians 3:12-15).

This is talking about two kinds of works. The first is the kind that survives fire (for example, gold, silver, precious stones, etc.). The second is that which does not survive fire, such as wood, hay, stubble, etc. In Matthew 25:14 we read the parable of a man traveling away to a far country who leaves money in the hands of his servants. He distributes to them each amounts *"according to their abilities."* One received five, another two, and the other one. When the master returned, he found that the one with five had worked with them and had made an additional five. The one with two had doubled his as well. However, the third had done nothing with what he had received. He had simply hidden it, so he would be able to give it back to the master when he returned. The master was unhappy with this, and he took the single amount from him and gave it to the one who had made five. In other words, each servant was rewarded with rulership over "things," many or few, depending on the profitability of the servant.

This parable makes clear that God requires fruitfulness from His servants. Non-fruitfulness results in being severed from the vine; and, on the judgment day, with losing even the gift that was originally given. The successful servants in this parable were considered "good and faithful." Thus, the definition of faithfulness, from God's point of view, isn't simply that you continue to follow Christ throughout your life, but that you are profitable with the gifts He has given you.

The reward of rulership is also consistent with another similar parable in Luke 19:11-27, a parable of rulership over cities. This could easily refer to our mission during the thousand-year "millennial Kingdom" on earth. The reward of work is more work. Yet, the honor, authority, and service to God in eternity will be through "ruling" with Him over His creation.

SCENE TWO: THRONE OF CHRIST'S GLORY

The second judgment scene takes place at a similar time to the first, but just before the millennium. This is called the throne of Christ's glory (see Matt. 25:31). The subject of judgment is those nations that will qualify to enter the millennial Kingdom of God. Matthew 25:31-46 tells us that *"all nations will be gathered before Him."* He will then "separate" the *"sheep from the goats."* He will make His judgments based on how they have treated His "brethren." If a nation ignored hunger, thirst, nakedness, sickness, imprisonment, and any other suffering in the lives of God's people, they will depart into *"everlasting punishment."* Those who attended to these needs will *"inherit the Kingdom prepared for you from the foundation of the world"* (Matt. 25:34). How this will actually happen is not explained, but it could be that nations that are judged may lose their boundaries and be simply amalgamated into those that receive the rewards.

It would seem that a more individual application of this parable is unavoidable. Each of us must care for those who suffer and bring them relief.

SCENE THREE: THE GREAT WHITE THRONE

The third scene of judgment is the most fearsome of all. There is no hope at all attached to this event. It is the great white throne revealed in the Book of Revelation:

> *Then I saw a great white throne and Him who sat on it, from whose face the earth and the heaven fled way. And there was*

found no place for them. And I saw the dead, small and great stand before God, and books were opened. And another book was opened which is the Book of Life. And the dead were judged according to their works, by the things which were written in the books. The sea gave up the dead who were in it, and death and Hades delivered up the dead who were in them. And they were judged, each one according to his works. Then death and Hades were cast into the lake of fire. This is the second death. And anyone not found written in the Book of Life was cast into the lake of fire (Revelation 20:11-15).

Those who are born again will not be present at this judgment. This is the judgment of the dead, who are unregenerate, who have been born "only once" (in the flesh), and thus will die twice (whereas those who have been born twice—of the flesh and then of the Spirit—will die only once). This judgment occurs at the end of the millennium.

FINAL VICTORY OVER SATAN

At this time, another incredible event takes place. Christ has reigned over all the earth for a thousand years. Satan has been confined to a bottomless pit (see Rev. 20:2) during this thousand years, but is:

...released from his prison and will go out to deceive the nations which are in the four corners of the earth, Gog and Magog, to gather them together to battle...and surrounded the camp of the saints and the beloved city. And fire came down from God out of heaven and devoured them (Revelation 20:7-9).

In this scene, after being imprisoned for a millennium, the devil still attempts to overthrow the throne of God by fomenting rebellion and mobilizing an attack on the Holy City, where the Lord is dwelling at this time. Incredibly, the devil is able to find recruits among those who have been under the glorious rule of Christ for a thousand years. There has been an entire absence of evil, as satan has been bound during the millennium. Even so, God obviously wishes there to be one final purging of the inhabitants of earth, and some are found wanting. This will not affect those believers who were raptured, received their resurrection bodies, had been rewarded, and are now eternal citizens of the heavenly city.

WIN THEM!

Whatever you are doing, remember, it's a *people* world. You're not building a great organization, company, or church. You're building a great people—and if you build them, they will build whatever you are building.

Win people all the time. Contact, communicate, and connect. Win people, for the person *"…who wins souls is wise"* (Prov. 11:30).

CONCLUSION

—

AT THE END OF **J**OHN 14:31, Jesus says to His disciples, *"Arise, let us go from here."* That is exactly what the purpose of these studies is, to enable you to arise and proceed with the business God has called you to.

When *repentance* has become established in your life, you acquire the gift, ability, and confidence to rid yourself of sin and its consequences. This will not depart from you unless you deliberately turn, "stiffen your neck," and harden your heart against God.

The "gift" of repentance is one of the most precious gifts available to us. Without it, we are unable to get right with God. We cannot correct our attitude. We cannot feel guilt over our sins. We cannot feel shame over evil. We cannot even resolve to cease from sin. Repentance is essential for the victorious Christian life. Every now and then, every believer stumbles and needs to get back into a correct relationship with the Father. This always begins with repentance.

Faith is essential to Christian living, for it is the reflection of what we are in Christ: bold, confident, assured, unafraid even of death. Faith walks in complete assurance from God's Word and is able to preach these certainties to an uneasy world.

The *baptisms* in water and in the Holy Ghost are essential for living in victory. The spiritual equation that takes place through water baptism is the death of the old nature and the birth of the new. The new self is the only one God will deal with. It is the only one qualified to be a partaker of the New Covenant. Keep in mind that these studies have not simply been for information. This knowledge must become action for it to be effective. The Baptism of the Holy Spirit is essential for every one of us believers so that we will become effective witnesses for Christ, able to minister the *spiritual gifts* and abilities of God to the needs around us.

The *laying on of hands* will plant gifts, callings, and qualities in your life.

The last two subjects covered, *resurrection* and *eternal judgment,* both have to do with the unseen world; either they are yet to come or are presently invisible. This is where a major amount of our Christian life is spent, dealing with the invisible.

With a mixture of exhilarating hope and reverential fear of the Judge of all, well-anchored in these first seven foundational principles of Christian living, you can look forward to the resurrection and the eternal life Jesus has given freely to you, and we can all say: *Arise, let us go from here* (John 14:31).

BIBLIOGRAPHY

Barclay, William. *Daily Study Bible*. Akron, OH: St. Andrews Press, 1955.

Berkhof, L. *Manual of Christian Doctrine*. Grand Rapids, MI: Erdmans Publishers, 1933.

Cartwright, Peter. *Backwoods Preacher*. London: Arthur Hall, Virtue and Co., 1862.

Finney, Charles. *Experiencing the Presence of God*. New Kensington, PA: Whitaker House Publishing, 2000.

Fleury, Claude, John Wesley, George Whitefield, and Daniel Rowland. *The Manners of the Antient Christians*. London: Felix Farley, 1749.

Garrett, Les. *Which Bible Can We Trust?* Gosnells, Perth, Australia: Christian Centre Press, March 1982.

Lion Handbook. *History of Christianity*. Lion Publishing, 1977.

Lloyd-Jones, Martyn. *Joy Unspeakable*. Shaw Books, 2007.

Jamieson, Fausset, and Brown. *Commentary on the Whole Bible.* Grand Rapids, MI: Zondervan, 1961.

Mackelvie, William, William Blair, and David Young. *Annals and Statistics of the United Presbyterian Church.* Edinburgh: Oliphant & Co., 1873.

Pearlman, Myer. *Knowing the Doctrines of the Bible.* Gospel Publishing House, 1937.

Prince, Derek. *Foundation Series, Volume 1: Sovereign World.* Charlotte, NC: Derek Prince Ministries Publishing, 1966.

Spurgeon, Charles Haddon. *Sermons of Rev. C.H. Spurgeon of London.* New York: Sheldon and Co., 1869.

Strong, James. *The New Strong's Complete Dictionary of Bible Words.* Thomas Nelson, 1996.

Unger, Merril. *Ungers Bible Dictionary.* Chicago: Moody Press, 1957.

Vine, W.E. *Expository Dictionary of New Testament Words.* Oliphants, 1940.

Young, Robert. *Young's Analytical Concordance to the Bible.* Hendrickson Publishers, 1984.

Wesley, John. *The Journal of the Rev. John Wesley: Vol. I.* London: J. Kershaw.

ABOUT PHIL PRINGLE

FOR THE PAST **30 YEARS,** Phil Pringle has been the senior pastor of C3 Church, one of Australia's fastest growing, largest, most exciting churches.

He has seen powerful moves of God break out, the glory of the Lord engulf the atmosphere, and people touched and permanently changed by the Holy Spirit.

Pastor Pringle earned his doctorate in biblical philosophy, and in 2000 was awarded the Order of Australia Medal by the government of Australia for his service to the Sydney community.

He has overseen the planting of new churches in major cities throughout the world. Today, there are nearly 300 C3 churches around the globe, which collectively make up C3 Church Global, with a combined membership of nearly 75,000.

In addition to its renowned teaching ministry, C3 has an internationally acclaimed, accredited education program that includes kindergarten through high school, and offers baccalaureate degrees in disciplines that include:

- The School of Ministry, which trains ministers and develops powerful ministries.

- The School of Creative Arts, focusing in all disciplines of the arts.

- The Pastoral Care and Counseling College.

- The International School of the Church, which trains pastors and teams to plant churches and take the Word of God to new levels of growth.

Pastor Pringle is also a renowned artist who works in oil and acrylic, and is the author of several books, including *Faith, Keys to Financial Excellence, Healing the Wounded Spirit, Top 10 Qualities of a Great Leader, But God, Dead for Nothing?* and *Inspired to Pray: The Art of Seeking God.*

He is currently working on his next book, *Letters to the Next Generation Leaders*, a contemporary commentary on First and Second Timothy, aimed at Christian leaders who are emerging from within today's young generation.

You may contact him through Michael McCall, President, CAM Artistic Management, at www.CAMArtisticManagement.com.